NO EASY ANSWERS

Christians Debate Nuclear Arms

Robert L. Spaeth

WINSTON PRESS

To Betty

The author wishes to express his gratitude to Annette Atkins, Jerome Eller, and Betty Spaeth for generous help with this book's form and content; to Lynda Fish, Linda Hanley, and Pamela Reding for expert secretarial assistance; and to Wayne Paulson, Cyril A. Reilly, and John Welshons of Winston Press for professional editorial assistance.

Cover design Art Direction Inc.

5 4 3 2

Winston Press, Inc.
430 Oak Grove
Minneapolis, Minnesota 55403

CONTENTS

68532

INTRODUCTION

As the 1980s opened, a great public debate erupted in the United States—a debate fraught with political, moral, and religious significance. The issue brings moral principles into confrontation with the nuclear armaments and the nuclear defense policies of the United States government. Are the weapons and the policies moral, or immoral? acceptable, or unacceptable? tolerable, or intolerable? Who will decide whether the weapons and policies should be supported or condemned? Politicians? Religious leaders? Philosophers? Theologians? Ordinary citizens? What actions should follow from moral judgments made about nuclear weapons and government defense policies?

Persons raising this issue into public prominence have been primarily religious leaders and thinkers from the Roman Catholic and Protestant communities. The questions they are asking have not been the typical social and political questions discussed throughout the nuclear age. Rather, moral and religious questioning has become the order of the day.

The specifically religious character of the nuclear debate is symbolized by the cover of *Time* magazine for November 29, 1982: The cover illustration depicts Joseph Bernardin, Roman Catholic archbishop of Chicago (since named a cardinal), clothed in a bishop's traditional religious vestments, including mitre. The cover headline reads, "God and the Bomb: Catholic Bishops Debate Nuclear Morality." Religion and morality have entered the public forum on this issue with such strength that no informed person can ignore them.

No new technological development in weaponry created the issue, although plans to build a new intercontinental missile (the so-called MX) and new delivery systems for missiles, including the Trident submarine, certainly contributed to its growth. No strikingly new government policies produced the

1

issue either. The administration of President Ronald Reagan for the most part continued defense policies of previous administrations, although the Reagan administration's efforts to improve the U.S. nuclear position relative to the Soviet Union definitely contributed to the prominence of the issue.

Rather than new weapons or new policies, the primary reason for the current prominence of debate on the morality of nuclear weapons is the evolving nature of religious leadership itself. American religious leaders are finding a new voice, a new confidence, a new determination to move American society toward peace in this deeply troubled nuclear age. The national meeting of Roman Catholic bishops that led to the *Time* cover story exemplified the new religious voices heard throughout the United States. Three hundred bishops met in the nation's capital in November 1982 to discuss the moral questions imbedded in the massive problems of war and peace in our age. They focused on a pastoral letter that would be sent to guide their community of fifty million American Catholics. Never in the past had a council of Roman Catholic bishops dealt with such an issue: The letter—then in its second draft—analyzed deterrence, first-strike policies, retaliation, tactical and strategic weapons, limited war, the military budget. Indeed, the document also included theological arguments and explicitly relied on Scripture for its most basic principles. Had the bishops been debating traditional theology, it is unlikely they would have caught the attention of the Reagan administration. But in fact the administration contributed to the bishops' proceedings in a way important enough to be reported in every major newspaper in the country.

Although Roman Catholic bishops became the most visible group among the religious voices raised anew on the question of the morality of nuclear armaments, other religious leaders and communities have been equally active, including the mainline Protestant churches of the United States. The effect of religious leadership has been felt across American society. In the November elections of 1982, for example, resolutions advocating a bilateral freeze on the production and deployment of nuclear weapons appeared on the ballots of eight states, the District of Columbia, and numerous counties and cities. Virtually all religious groups expressing a judgment supported the freeze. And freeze referenda won voters' approval in seven of eight states, the District of Columbia, and several large metropolitan areas.

The issue of the morality of nuclear weapons is one of grim seriousness, for the weapons and delivery systems of the United States, the Soviet Union, and several other nations have horrendous possibilities for destruction. All religious leaders entering this debate have called attention to the seriousness of the matter, whatever their conclusions or recommendations. In a 1980 pastoral letter, the House of Bishops of the Episcopal Church gave its understanding of what is at stake:

> Since nuclear armaments here and in the Soviet Union have created a world in which the whole can nowhere be protected against its parts, our own national security has reached the zero point. The issue is no longer the survival of one nation against another. We stand now in mortal danger of global human incineration.[1]

In 1981 the Lutheran World Federation Executive Committee deplored the "spread of dread, fear and resignation among peoples" caused by the nuclear arms race (*Lutheran World Information*, 20 Aug. 1981, p. 14). The responses people are making to this issue come from the human depths where religious and moral principles move the mind and heart. Consequently, the judgments and opinions rendered by religious leaders and ordinary citizens alike have tended to be filled with commitment, fervor, even passion. Raymond Hunthausen, Roman Catholic archbishop of Seattle, exhibited this passion when he said in 1981, "Our nuclear war preparations are the global crucifixion of Jesus" (*National Catholic Reporter*, 12 Feb. 1982). Leaders and others moved deeply by their beliefs about the dangers of nuclear weapons have expressed their feelings about the issue in many ways, from public prayer to picketing, from speeches to demonstrations.

But neither discussions nor demonstrations have generated a consensus. Disagreement abounds—on the moral and religious bases for judgments about policies and weapons, on the reasoning needed to understand the questions raised by the issue, on the recommendations that might be made to governments here and abroad, on the means appropriate to bring the issue to the attention of people at large.

How can interested and concerned, but possibly perplexed, people decide for themselves what are reasonable answers to the myriad of problems raised by nuclear weapons? There is no lack of books, articles, media presentations, live speeches, or discussions. No American can plead ignorance on the grounds that information is unavailable. Yet the books and speeches and films are almost invariably presented by people who have already reached definite conclusions and wish to argue in support of their own judgments. They seek to persuade more than to enlighten.

Religious leaders—ministers or priests or theologians or assemblies—usually direct their remarks to co-religionists, calling for agreement based on a common understanding of the faith. Prayer services, moreover, are designed to encourage a sense of community. When moral statements about nuclear weapons or policies are made in such a context, the assembled faithful are urged by both the words and the setting to agree with the opinions and sentiments expressed. Churches have seldom resembled debating societies, and the pastoral approach of priests and ministers seldom encourages dissent from pastoral exhortations.

Yet since the issue of the morality of nuclear weapons touches on politics as well as morality, it arouses public controversy always and everywhere. For Americans, controversy on political subjects signals the need and opportunity to make up their own minds. Moreover, the independence fostered by political thinking and social action differs in kind from the shared beliefs of a religious congregation. Difficult political issues in the United States rarely generate a consensus, even among individuals who gather together because of shared principles.

So even political party meetings are characterized by disagreement more than by agreement.

Thus a responsible person, thinking about an issue simultaneously religious, moral, and political, tends to be pulled in several directions at once. One might tend to think one way because of previous political opinions, yet another way because of religious beliefs. One might want to reach one's own judgments, yet be accustomed to specific guidance from church or priest or minister.

The morality of nuclear weapons and policies is definitely such a divisive and confusing issue. Everyone is urged to agree with this or that religious position or follow this or that political leader. An editor of *The New Republic*, Leon Wieseltier, has written that the extremes of the debate tend to command most of the public's attention: "The citizens of this nation . . . are trapped between visionaries and experts. They are given sermons or systems analysis" ("The Great Nuclear Debate," *The New Republic*, 10 and 17 Jan. 1983, p. 8). Citizens are told that certain conclusions should be adopted because nuclear war would be unimaginably horrible, because the Soviet leaders cannot be trusted, because the world is sliding toward all-out war, because the United States is an inferior world power, because our religion—whatever it may be—demands our commitment to peace in this way or that. No one can decide these questions simply or easily, yet responsible persons believe they must make the effort.

The depth of feeling of those who have made commitments on the nuclear weapons-morality issue has heated up the rhetoric of the debate. A Jesuit theologian, the Reverend Richard McSorley of Georgetown University, wrote an influential article in 1976 entitled "It's a Sin to Build a Nuclear Weapon." William E. McManus, Roman Catholic bishop of Fort Wayne, Indiana, has urged that, in the nuclear age, Christians "ought to embrace [the] Gospel teaching for sanity in a world verging on madness" (Heyer, *Key Statements*, p. 215). A theological commission of the Reformed Church in America has called the nuclear arms race "first and foremost a false religion" (ibid., p. 266). Belief raised to passion and inflamed by rhetoric creates a still more difficult context for those who wish to think for themselves.

This book does not intend to add yet another voice to those urging Americans to think one way or another on the nuclear weapons-morality issue; it does not reach conclusions of which it seeks to persuade its readers. Rather, it offers information, reviews issues, and discusses moral perspectives. This book assumes that American citizens, properly informed, are capable of making good decisions on difficult social and moral issues. To that end the book contains chapters on the history of nuclear weapons and policies, on the most prominent moral issues connected with nuclear armaments, and on the moral perspectives that leaders and other citizens bring to bear on the issues. Religious leaders have a prominent place in the book because they have carried most of the debate in the 1980s. Roman Catholic leaders in particular are quoted frequently, not because their views are the most important but because those views have often occupied the center of the stage of public debate in recent years.

This book also assumes that people of good will do intend to do their part to prevent war, nuclear war most of all, and that all responsible citizens are peacemakers in their hearts. Thus the emphasis in the book falls on the reasons advanced to support conclusions about how to achieve peace in our time. The pastoral letter of the National Conference of Catholic Bishops, *The Challenge of Peace*, points out: "People may agree in abhorring an injustice, for instance, yet sincerely disagree as to what practical approach will achieve justice."[2] This book takes for granted that such a situation prevails on the issue of nuclear armaments and nuclear defense policies: We Americans disagree widely and deeply about what people and governments should do, even though we share with all our strength the conviction that nuclear war must be avoided.

David W. Preus, president of the American Lutheran Church, has urged careful thinking on the issues of nuclear weapons and morality for all church members:

> Informed and morally based public opinion is imperative in a nuclear age. The setting of policy should not be the work of government leaders and nuclear experts alone. We are all involved, and it is important that the churches contribute their best thinking and that church people get deeply engaged in the public debate that determines nuclear weapons policy. ("Help Determine Nuclear Weapons Policy," *The Lutheran Standard*, 21 Jan. 1983, p. 29)

The information, history, issues, and perspectives presented in this book cannot definitively settle any part of the grave moral concerns engendered by nuclear weapons. No authority is reliable enough to do that job either.

Nevertheless, as Christians fervently pursue the debate and define the moral issues, political leaders must make choices here and now about the production, deployment, and use of nuclear arms.

Former United States Senator Eugene J. McCarthy has written of the special responsibility for rational and moral judgment in political action:

> Faith is, of course, no full and automatic substitute for knowledge and intelligence, although the truths of faith should, when applied to contemporary problems, have some bearing upon the understanding and upon the solution of human problems. The religious character of a people should be reflected in its social and political institutions and actions. . . .
>
> Knowledge of the Bible, the Koran, the Ten Commandments, or of the spiritual and corporal works of mercy does not . . . give the religious man in politics a ready answer to all problems. . . .
>
> Politics is a part of the real world. In politics the simple choice between that which is wholly right and that which is wholly wrong is seldom given; the ideal is not often

realized and in some cases cannot even be advo-
cated. . . . The choice involved is not one of the lesser
of two evils, really, but the choice of that course which
has some good in it, or promise of good, no matter how
limited. Prudence may require the toleration of a measure
of evil in order to prevent something worse, or to save
a limited good.[3]

There seems to be no alternative but thinking through the
complex and difficult issues for ourselves as well as we can.
There are no easy answers.

PART ONE

Background

1

THE NUCLEAR ERA OPENS

The 1940s and 1950s

On July 16, 1945, when the world's first nuclear explosion shattered earth and air in southern New Mexico, the human race came to possess an awesome destructive power and simultaneously created the most intractable moral problem of the contemporary world. Three weeks later the new weapon was used in war at Hiroshima, Japan. But controversy over its moral status and its future risks had already begun, and it continues to the present time. Argument among scientists, public officials, philosophers, theologians, and concerned persons in all walks of life over the morality of nuclear arms has escalated as rapidly as the danger itself.

Two months after Japan's surrender ended World War II, J. Robert Oppenheimer anticipated the intensity of the forthcoming debate over nuclear weapons. "If atomic bombs are to be added to the arsenals of a warring world or to the arsenals of nations preparing for war," he said, "then the time will come when mankind will curse the names of Los Alamos and Hiroshima."[1] A physicist and the director of the Los Alamos Scientific Laboratory, where the first nuclear bombs were developed, Oppenheimer took an important part in the debate over using the new weapon in the war against Japan. (Nazi Germany had surrendered before the New Mexico test.) Participants in the first nuclear-morality debate included eminent scientists and high-ranking public officials with grave wartime responsibilities.

Even before the test explosion in July, President Harry S Truman had appointed an Interim Committee to consider, among other things, the moral acceptability of using the still-unknown weapon in the war. Secretary of War Henry L. Stimson presided, and Oppenheimer served on an advisory scientific panel. The scientific panel was asked to consider whether a demonstration explosion of an atomic bomb might be feasible and perhaps sufficient to bring the war to an end. According to a later account by Arthur H. Compton, also a member of the panel, most of the scientists who worked on the bomb's development agreed with the panel's recommendation in June of 1945 that "no technical demonstration [is] likely to bring an end to the war; we see no acceptable alternative to direct military use."[2] But Leo Szilard, a physicist who had helped persuade Albert Einstein to warn President Franklin D. Roosevelt in 1939 of the possibilities of atomic weapons, opposed military use of the new bomb on moral grounds. Szilard circulated a petition among knowledgeable scientists claiming that once the weapons were used "it would be difficult to resist the temptation" to use them again, and that a nation using them "may have to bear the responsibility of opening the door to an era of destruction on an unimaginable scale" (Compton, *Atomic Quest*, p. 242).

But such argumentation against the atomic bomb's use in the war aroused opposition from those worried about the great loss of American lives expected in an invasion of Japan. Secretary Stimson estimated that a million casualties might be sustained by American armed forces before Japan would surrender. Compton had polled 150 members of the Metallurgical Laboratory at the University of Chicago—where the first self-sustaining nuclear chain reaction had been achieved in 1942—on the question of the bomb's use. Eighty-seven percent voted for military use.

The decision to drop the bomb over Japan was made by President Truman. In late July of 1945 the president attended an Allied conference at Potsdam, which included the United States, the Soviet Union, Great Britain, and China. On July 26 the conference issued a joint declaration, the last paragraph of which hinted at the existence of the new weapon:

> We call upon the government of Japan to proclaim now
> the unconditional surrender of all Japanese armed forces,
> and to provide proper and adequate assurances of their
> good faith in such action. The alternative for Japan is
> prompt and utter destruction.[3]

No more explicit warning to the Japanese about new weapons of war was given. On August 6, an atomic bomb—made from uranium and deriving its energy from fission of uranium nuclei—was dropped and exploded over Hiroshima with the force of more than 20,000 tons of TNT. The city was razed almost instantly, and over 70,000 people were killed. A second fission bomb—made from the artificial element plutonium— was dropped on Nagasaki on August 9 and killed more than 40,000 people. The Japanese government surrendered the next day.

Moral debate over the use of nuclear weapons has centered on whether such destructive weapons should ever be used and, if they are to be used in war, what sort of targets are morally acceptable. President Truman answered both of these questions firmly. In his memoirs, he recalled his decision to authorize the use of the bomb in Japan:

> I regarded the bomb as a military weapon and never had
> any doubt that it should be used . . . In deciding to use
> this bomb I wanted to make sure that it would be used
> as a weapon of war in the manner prescribed by the laws
> of war. That meant I wanted it dropped on a military
> target.[4]

Moral anguish over the dangers of atomic weapons increased soon after the war, as a much more powerful bomb—deriving its energy from the fusion of heavy-hydrogen nuclei—was being developed. By this time international tensions between the U.S. and the U.S.S.R.—allies in the war—were severe. The U.S.S.R. forcibly installed puppet governments in eastern European countries and attempted to isolate Berlin from the

Allied occupation zones in western Germany. In 1950, when the armed forces of North Korea—with the sanction of the Soviets—invaded South Korea, the U.S. entered another war.

The new fusion bomb—called the H-bomb or the super-bomb—was not only more powerful than the fission A-bomb, but there was theoretically no upper limit to the magnitude of its explosive power. The Manhattan Project on the A-bomb was a crash program with high wartime priority. In the immediate postwar years, while the U.S. had a monopoly on atomic bombs, there was no pressing need to launch a production program for the H-bomb. Then, slightly over four years after the end of the war—on August 29, 1949—the Soviet Union exploded a nuclear weapon of the fission type.

From its inception in 1946 the Atomic Energy Commission had sought scientific advice from its General Advisory Committee (GAC), which was now called upon to make a recommendation concerning the potential development of the H-bomb. The Chairman of the GAC was J. Robert Oppenheimer. In its report of October 1949, the committee pointed out that "this weapon would bring about the destruction of innumerable human lives; it is not a weapon which can be used exclusively for the destruction of material installations of military or semi-military purposes."[5] The committee concluded that the H-bomb should not be developed.

Committee members explained their reasons for the negative recommendation in two addenda to the report—the first signed by Oppenheimer and five other scientists, the second by physicists Enrico Fermi and I. I. Rabi. In retrospect, the differences between the arguments of the two addenda seem small in comparison with the similarities. Of special contemporary interest is the fact that the two statements foreshadow most of the moral issues persisting in the controversy over use of nuclear weapons.

The Oppenheimer addendum noted at the outset that the H-bomb could be expected to be 100 to 1000 times as powerful as the atomic bombs then in existence, and that it would spread its damage over an area 20 to 100 times as large as the area

damaged at Hiroshima. Oppenheimer and the others explained
their opposition to such weapons:

> We base our recommendation on our belief that the ex-
> treme dangers to mankind inherent in the proposal wholly
> outweigh any military advantage that could come from
> this development. Let it be clearly realized that this is a
> super weapon; it is in a totally different category from
> an atomic bomb. The reason for developing such super
> bombs would be to have the capacity to devastate a vast
> area with a single bomb. Its use would involve a decision
> to slaughter a vast number of civilians. We are alarmed
> as to the possible global effects of the radioactivity gen-
> erated by the explosion of a few super bombs of con-
> ceivable magnitude. If super bombs will work at all, there
> is no inherent limit in the destructive power that may be
> attained with them. Therefore, a super bomb might be-
> come a weapon of genocide.
>
> The existence of such a weapon in our armory would
> have far-reaching effects on world opinion; reasonable
> people the world over would realize that the existence of
> a weapon of this type whose power of destruction is
> essentially unlimited represents a threat to the future of
> the human race which is intolerable. Thus we believe
> that the psychological effect of the weapon in our hands
> would be adverse to our interest.
>
> We believe a super bomb should never be produced.
> (York, *Advisors*, pp. 156-57)

The addendum of Fermi and Rabi employed similar arguments and anticipated yet more of the later debate:

> It is clear that the use of such a weapon cannot be justified
> on any ethical ground which gives a human being a cer-
> tain individuality and dignity even if he happens to be a
> resident of an enemy country. . . . Its use would put the
> United States in a bad moral position relative to the peo-
> ples of the world.

. . . We believe it important for the President of the
United States to tell the American public, and the world,
that we think it wrong on fundamental ethical principles
to initiate a program of development of such a weapon.
(Pp. 158-59)

Both addenda to the GAC report recognized a potential
military threat from the Soviet Union; both said that in the
event of a war with the U.S.S.R., military retaliation employing the current U.S. stockpile of atomic (fission) bombs
would be sufficient.

The commissioners of the AEC were divided on the GAC's
recommendation. Commissioner Lewis Strauss strongly favored the production of the H-bomb. He wrote to President
Truman:

I believe that the United States must be completely armed
as any possible enemy. From this, it follows that I believe
it unwise to renounce, unilaterally, any weapon which an
enemy can reasonably be expected to possess. I recommend that the President direct the Atomic Energy Commission to proceed with the development of the ther-
monuclear bomb, at highest priority. . . . (Ibid., pp.
58-59)

Senator Brien McMahon of Connecticut, chairman of the
Congressional Joint Committee on Atomic Energy, brought
the argument in favor of the H-bomb closer to the perceived
Soviet threat: "If we let Russians get the super first, catastrophe
becomes all but certain—whereas, if we get it first, there exists
a chance of saving ourselves" (ibid., p. 60).

Final decision again fell to President Truman. Faced with
divided advice from the AEC, the President turned to the
Special Committee of the National Security Council, com-
posed of Secretary of State Dean Acheson, Secretary of Defense Louis Johnson, and AEC Chairman David Lilienthal.
They unanimously recommended going ahead with the hydro-
gen-bomb program. On January 31, 1951, President Truman

issued a public statement, in which he said:

It is part of my responsibility as Commander-in-Chief of
the armed forces to see to it that our country is able to
defend itself against any possible aggressor.

Accordingly, I have directed the Atomic Energy Commission to continue its work on all forms of atomic weapons, including the so-called hydrogen or super-bomb.[6]

The Soviet Union's collusion in the North Korean aggression against South Korea had confirmed the belief that the
U.S.S.R. was dangerous to world peace. Controversy over the
morality of nuclear weapons was now inseparable from the
dangers to peace posed by the Soviet government.

The U.S. exploded a test version of an H-bomb in the Pacific
Ocean on November 1, 1952. Its force was equivalent to that
of 10 million tons of TNT; in other words, it was almost 1000
times as powerful as the fission bombs of World War II. Less
than a year later, in August 1953, the Soviet Union exploded
an H-bomb. The arms race had begun.

Because of wartime secrecy and classification of technical
information about new weaponry, much of the debate in the
1940s over the morality of the A-bomb and the H-bomb was
conducted in inner circles, not in the public arena. Secret
information known only to public officials and atomic scientists
necessarily limited knowledgeable debate to these two groups.
The grave professional responsibilities of politicians, military
leaders, and scientists may have contributed to more competent
judgment, but the debate undoubtedly suffered from the ab-
sence of philosophers, theologians, humanists, and other ac-
ademic specialists. Moreover, the secrecy shielding much of
the controversy prevented real public discussion about the morality of nuclear weapons.

When the question became public, some of the same disagreements that had divided scientists and the AEC now divided other thinkers. A typical difference of opinion—this one
on the theological level—appeared in 1950 in the pages of
Commonweal, a weekly journal edited by Roman Catholic lay

persons ("The A-Bomb: Moral or Not?", 29 Sept. 1950, pp. 606-08). The Reverend Francis J. Connell, C.SS.R., dean of the School of Sacred Theology at Catholic University, publicly said that an atomic weapon "is not essentially different from a TNT bomb, a cannon, a hand grenade or a rifle." Gordon C. Zahn, a sociologist and Catholic pacifist leader, replied that an "essential distinction between the A-bomb and rifle must be recognized and our moral judgments revised accordingly." Zahn believed that if this distinction were not recognized and appreciated, then Americans would "abandon the traditional concepts of the intrinsic value and dignity of the redeemed human person and accept in its stead the *totaller Krieg* [total war] philosophy which treats of whole cities and their inhabitants as an impersonal mass."

In a rejoinder to Zahn, Connell said that distinctions between weapons themselves did not solve the moral problems of war with or without nuclear weapons. Some targets for an atomic bomb could be morally lawful, he wrote, such as "the destruction by atomic weapons of the enemy's A-bomb plant in a remote mountain region." But, Connell argued, "it is against God's law to employ any weapon of war directly against noncombatants." Connell had applied this principle to the attack on Hiroshima: "On the very day that the A-bomb was dropped on Hiroshima, I issued a public statement containing a condemnation of its use on this occasion because of the large number of non-combatants involved in the destruction."

This disagreement between two thoughtful Roman Catholics poses the question whether it is the nature of the new weapons or whether it is their possible uses that is the more significant morally. Zahn and Connell disagreed on the answer, but their debate occurred in 1950 before the H-bomb had been built and before Oppenheimer had expressed his view (quoted above) that an H-bomb "is in a totally different category from an atomic bomb."

By the mid-1950s the moral distinction between the fission and fusion bombs was moot. Development of smaller, so-called tactical fusion weapons along with huge, so-called strategic weapons revived the distinction, but the question whether nuclear weapons ought to be built at all was also moot. However, it would reappear in another form in the movement to demolish existing nuclear weapons. By the mid-1950s—as the Soviet Union proved capable of the same weapons research and development as the United States—the connection between nuclear weapons and big-power hostility was strongly, perhaps irreversibly, made.

Thus, within a decade after the first atomic explosion, moral thinking was forced to deal not only with the frightening possibility of the use of nuclear weapons but with the more frightening fact of their possession by two great world powers engaged in hostile ideological confrontation. In this geopolitical climate, extreme positions gained more approval than they would have in more settled times. Fear of Soviet intentions led some to favor an American threat of massive retaliation for any act of Russian aggression. Others, holding to traditional pacifism, denounced all war and any use of nuclear weapons.

Moral concern over the growth of nuclear armaments naturally involved political considerations, since two powerful governments possessed the weapons. But the moral concern was given a more personal dimension as the actual human suffering already caused by the fission bombs dropped on Japan entered the public debate. *Hiroshima,* a powerful and emotional report on six survivors of the first atomic bomb, written by John Hersey, was published in *The New Yorker* in 1946. One of the survivors was a German Jesuit priest, Father Wilhelm Kleinsorge. After the war, the Jesuits in Hiroshima had discussed the moral questions raised by the atomic bomb. Hersey quotes one Jesuit's report to the Vatican:

Some of us consider the bomb in the same category as poison gas and were against its use on a civilian population. Others were of the opinion that in total war, as carried on in Japan, there was no difference between civilians and soldiers, and that the bomb itself was an effective force tending to end the bloodshed, warning Japan to surrender and thus to avoid total destruction. It seems logical that he who supports total war in principle cannot complain of a war against civilians. The crux of the matter is whether total war in its present form is justifiable, even when it serves a just purpose. Does it not have material and spiritual evil as its consequences which far exceed whatever good might result? When will our moralists give us a clear answer to this question?[7]

Pope Pius XII, in his Easter message of 1954, announced his determination to "tirelessly endeavor to bring about, by means of international agreements—always in subordination to the principle of legitimate self-defense—the effective proscription and banishment of atomic, biological and chemical warfare" (*The Catholic Mind,* July 1954, p. 439). In a speech to the World Medical Congress five months later, Pius made his ethical stand on atomic weapons clearer. He questioned whether the use of such weapons was "permissible as a matter of principle" in view of "the untold horror and suffering induced by modern warfare." He answered cautiously. First, he said, "to launch such a war other than on just grounds" (defined as "an obvious, extremely serious, and otherwise unavoidable violation of justice") would be a most serious breach of moral principle. He stressed that the question of the lawful use of nuclear weapons (along with biological and chemical weapons) could not even legitimately be asked unless one assumed that they would be used only "when it is deemed absolutely necessary as a means of self-defense." Even then, he said, "every effort must be made to avert [the use of such weapons] through international agreements."

Pius added a special concern: If control over the use of nuclear weapons is lost, then their use "should be rejected as immoral." In such a case, he argued, the question becomes one of "the pure and simple annihilation of human life within the radius of action. Under no circumstances is this to be permitted" (Heyer, *Key Statements*, p. 14).

Rather than providing the clear answer hoped for by the Hiroshima Jesuits, the pope's remarks raised other questions for interpretation and dispute. For example, although the pope had tied his condemnation of "pure and simple annihilation" to a loss of control of the new weapons, a prominent British theologian, F. H. Drinkwater, saw it as a condemnation of the use of H-bombs in populated areas without reference to control of targeting ("The Morality of Nuclear War," *Commonweal*, 18 March 1955, pp. 623-27).

A still more complex and deeper question—that of justice in modern war—was raised anew by Pius's remarks, and this drew the sustained attention of Father John Courtney Murray, S.J., a subtle and persuasive American theologian. In a 1958 address to the Catholic Association for International Peace on the themes of Pius's thought, he rejected the extreme positions on the question. One extreme, he said, is "relative Christian pacifism," which argues that "no adequate justification can be offered for the ruinous effects of today's weapons of war"; the other extreme argues that since "Communism, as an ideology and as a power-system, constitutes the gravest possible menace to the moral and civilizational values that form the basis of 'the West,'" the West should "be prepared to use any means that promise success." Murray held that neither of these positions "squared with the public doctrine of the Church."

Between "the false extremes of pacifism and bellicism," Murray said, lies the solution to the problem of justice in modern war. The extremes lead to the dilemma of "desperate alternatives, either universal atomic death or complete surrender to Communism." Murray found this dilemma "an abdication of the moral reason and a craven submission to some manner of technological or historical determinism."

The middle ground, Murray argued, contains the concept of "limited war." Limited war is the only policy that makes it possible to avoid the "desperate alternatives." Limitation of war should thus become the moral goal of policymakers, who ought to use as "the principle of limitation" the "exigencies of legitimate defense against injustice" (*Theological Studies,* March 1959, pp. 40-61 passim).

This was the state of the public debate over the morality of nuclear weapons at the close of the 1950s.

Discussion Questions

Note: These questions are intended to stimulate thought, discussion, and further reading and reflection. Most of them implicitly urge the reader to "explain your position" or "support your beliefs." The questions illustrate that, as the title of this book suggests, there are no easy answers to the moral difficulties posed by nuclear weapons.

1. Leo Szilard said in 1945 that any nation using nuclear weapons might have to "bear the responsibility of opening the door to an era of destruction on an unimaginable scale." What kinds of destruction might nuclear warfare cause?
2. The United States is the only nation to have used nuclear arms in warfare. Does this fact give the U.S. a special responsibility to prevent future use of such weapons?
3. Nuclear weapons have not been used in war since 1945. Does this fact reassure you that they will not be used in the near future?
4. President Harry S Truman considered Hiroshima "a military target" for the first atomic bomb. Are there any conditions under which an entire city could properly be called a military target?
5. How might the world be different if the United States had followed the advice of J. Robert Oppenheimer in 1949 that the H-bomb "should never be produced"?
6. Pope Pius XII in 1954 expressed concern about chemical, biological, and atomic weapons. Why did he single out these kinds of weapons? Do you agree with the view that nuclear war is qualitatively different from other forms of war?

2

MISSILES AND NEGOTIATIONS

The 1960s and 1970s

When the first atomic and hydrogen bombs were built, the only way to deliver them to military targets was by airplane. But a far swifter and more accurate device came into production and prominence in the late 1950s: the intercontinental ballistic missile (ICBM). A nuclear explosive attached as a warhead to an ICBM capable of traveling thousands of miles and led to its target by internal guidance mechanisms became the most deadly weapon in all of military history.

The United States and the Soviet Union both developed guided missiles, and both continue to improve and expand the missiles' capabilities. The U.S. tested its first ICBM, the Atlas, in 1958; the second, the Titan, a year later. Both were liquid-fueled rockets. In 1961, the first American solid-fueled ICBM, the Minuteman, was launched from an underground silo. The new problem of defending these missile silos against possible enemy attack became an important strategic military consideration in the continuing debate over the morality of nuclear weapons.

By 1960 the U.S. had built and tested the Polaris missile, which could be fired from a submerged submarine at sea. In subsequent models of both land-based and sea-based missiles, the destructive power of the warheads was increased greatly. Furthermore, the Poseidon (successor to the Polaris) and the Minuteman III were equipped to carry several bombs that could be sent to separate targets. These missiles were known as multiple independently targeted reentry vehicles (MIRVs).

With Soviet development of both bombs and missiles, the U.S. needed to protect missile silos against potential nuclear attack. This need led to an emphasis on the ability to launch more American missiles from mobile, difficult-to-detect submarines. Throughout the late 1950s and early 1960s, the American policy of massive retaliation asserted that in the event of a Soviet attack on the U.S. or its allies, our government would authorize and launch a huge retaliatory attack on the U.S.S.R., including its populated areas.

This so-called counter-city strategy was altered during the administration of President John F. Kennedy (1961-63) to a counter-force strategy. Secretary of Defense Robert McNamara defined the change in nuclear policy in 1962:

> The United States has come to the conclusion that, to the extent feasible, basic military strategy in a possible nuclear war should be approached in much the same way that more conventional military operations have been regarded in the past. That is to say, principal military objectives, in the event of a nuclear war stemming from an attack on the Alliance, should be the destruction of the enemy's forces, not of his civilian population.[1]

The distinction between a counter-city and a counter-force strategy is basic for those for whom the various possible uses of nuclear weapons constitute the crucial moral question. For those who declare all uses of nuclear weapons to be morally repugnant, however, the distinction either lacks significance or else is pernicious, since an American counter-force strategy may tempt our country to use such nuclear weapons.

Paul Ramsey, a Protestant theologian and Professor of Christian Ethics at Princeton University, expressed astonishment that "decent citizens of this country, Christian and non-Christian," did not respond to the new counter-force strategy with "a chorus of 'Amens!'" As his own response, Professor Ramsey wrote the previously mentioned booklet, *The Limits of Nuclear War,* in which he defended the thesis that "counter-force nuclear war is the upper limit of rational, politically purposive military action" (pp. 7, 10).

Ramsey argued strongly against the view held by some, that "since war as such is immoral, no *moral* judgments can be made concerning the way it is conducted." If it is nuclear war in particular that is condemned as immoral as such, then Ramsey had anticipated (and opposed) much of later anti-nuclear armaments thinking (p. 15).

Ramsey judged all-out nuclear war to be beyond moral condemnation and called it irrational, even insane. A nuclear attack limited to a few cities, he said, "partakes of the same insanity" (p. 22). The question for American citizens then becomes how to prevent such war.

Ramsey examined the two extreme positions on this question. At one extreme are the pacifists, who favor total disarmament—or at least total nuclear disarmament—on the grounds that all armed conflicts in a nuclear age are immoral. At the other extreme are the military strategists who claim to prevent nuclear war with policies that threaten massive attacks against enemy populations; they even go to the extent of proposing that U.S. nuclear weapons be built to be launched automatically, to convince the enemy that we mean business.

Ramsey argued against both extremes with a proposed policy that imagines the real possibility of nuclear war, then sets about to find ways to limit it. "Only if fighting a possible war is understood to be a governing purpose of a military establishment will inherent limits in the design of war seem choiceworthy" (p. 11).

A counter-force strategy, according to this view, would meet a major requirement of just war: the prohibition of deliberate attack upon noncombatants; and still the nation would be able to defend itself against potential aggression. Ramsey proposed specific policies that would be consistent with this understanding of what is rational and moral in the nuclear age. U.S. forces able to fight nonnuclear war—so-called conventional war—should be increased, Ramsey argued. The U.S. should announce that "we will never be the first to use nuclear weapons—*except* tactical ones that may and will be used against forces only and not strategically against an enemy's heartland, to stop an invasion across a clearly defined boundary" (p. 32). And, in general, U.S. nuclear armaments "must be maintained for use in counterforce strikes over an enemy's territory" (p. 38).

Two decades after Paul Ramsey's booklet appeared, a new debate arose over the justice of a deterrent force, that is, a U.S. nuclear weapons system deployed for the purpose of deterring the Soviet Union from a nuclear attack on the U.S. or its allies. Ramsey saw the morality of deterrence as follows. On the one hand, he argued, "If deterrence rests upon intending massive retaliation, it is clearly wrong no matter how much peace results." On the other hand, our very possession of nuclear weapons may serve as a deterrent to the Russians; but this possibility raises the question of whether our possession of the weapons is tantamount to intending the very massive retaliation deserving condemnation. Here Ramsey asks a more difficult question: "whether 'possession' of massive nuclear weapons is reducible to the crime of 'using' them over civilian targets . . . whether 'having' or 'possession' implies a criminal intention to use them murderously, or a conditional willingness to do so. . . ." To this critical question Ramsey answered that "the weapons themselves will continue to have deterrent effects because they have ambiguous [i.e., counterforce or counter-city] uses" and that "*apart from intention* their capacity to deter cannot be removed from them" (pp. 46-49).

Ramsey summarized his moral understanding of deterrence as follows:

The crucial question for the moralist is whether deterrent effects that flow from a *specified kind* of studied ambiguity concerning the intention with which a nation holds nuclear weapons in reserve are *praeter intentionem* (besides or without the actual intention to attack cities). . . .

To say and to act as if we might go to city exchanges is certainly a form of deception. But, if this can be done

without intending to make irrational immoral use of nuclear weapons, and even with the intention that our weapons be not so used and with the intention of revoking
what had never even the appearance of total committal,
such deception cannot be said to be based on the criminal
intention or conditional willingness to do murder. The
first thing to be said then, is that the intention to deceive
is certainly a far cry from the intention to murder society,
or to commit mutual homicide. (P. 51)

In 1963, Sylvester P. Theisen, a sociologist on the faculty
of St. John's University (Minnesota), explored the nuclear
question, using Roman Catholic sources. Writing in *The American Benedictine Review,* he relied more explicitly than Ramsey
on the philosophy of just war, which Theisen said is part of
the "scholastic moral philosophy of the Catholic Church."
According to this prescription, "there are a number of conditions which must *all* be satisfied if a war is to be morally
justifiable." Theisen listed them:

1. The cause must be just.
2. The war must be made by a lawful authority.
3. The intention of the government declaring war must
   be just.
4. War must be the only possible means of securing
   justice.
5. Only right means may be employed in the conduct of
   the war.
6. There must be reasonable hope of victory.
7. The good probably to be achieved by victory must
   outweigh the probable evil effects of the war.
   ("Man and Nuclear Weapons," Sept. 1963, p. 373)

Theisen put the question squarely: "Can a nuclear war of
any kind ever be genuinely justifiable in terms of [these] conditions?" (ibid.). Certain forms of nuclear war, he argued, can
never be so justified, such as "all-out nuclear attack upon
population centers. But in a limited defensive war for limited

objectives," Theisen decided, "the eventual use of limited nuclear war can be morally permitted in terms of the seven conditions" of a just war (ibid., p. 376).

In the sometimes barbarous world of international relations, Theisen argued, "immutable moral rules"—such as just-war criteria—"must take lower, more primitive forms. . . . barbarous circumstances allow the use, in fact demand the use, of coercive means which would not be permitted in a law-abiding world society" (ibid.). Theisen further argued that a nuclear force coupled to a policy decision to counterattack nuclear aggression by an enemy nation "will help maintain peace through mutual terror until a sounder, more durable peace can be established through other means." To potential opponents of this position, Theisen replied: "Peace through a balance of terror is something less than that tranquility of order philosophers envisage or the reign of love religious men pray for, but at least it is not nuclear war" (ibid., p. 379).

Pope John XXIII added his influential voice to the concern over nuclear weapons morality in 1963 in his widely discussed encyclical *Pacem in Terris*. Addressing himself to the entire world, the pope called upon all people to adopt the principle that "the true and solid peace of nations consists not in equality of arms but in mutual trust alone."[2] The most direct statement on nuclear weapons in *Pacem in Terris* is:

> Justice, . . . right reason and humanity urgently demand that the arms race should cease; that the stockpiles which exist in various countries should be reduced equally and simultaneously by the parties concerned; that nuclear weapons should be banned; and that a general agreement should eventually be reached about progressive disarmament and an effective method of control. (P. 39)

Two years later the Second Vatican Council used a phrase that has reverberated in virtually every subsequent debate on nuclear-weapons morality. This phrase appeared in the Council's pastoral letter, *Pastoral Constitution on the Church in the Modern World,* in which the assembled bishops of the Roman

Catholic Church recommended that war be evaluated "with an entirely new attitude." The new attitude was not defined. Following this provocative phrase, the bishops condemned counter-city nuclear warfare as "a crime against God and man himself" and warned that the balance of armaments is not a "sure and authentic peace" but rather that "the arms race is an utterly treacherous trap for humanity" (Heyer, *Key Statements*, pp. 19-20).

As moral and religious concern over nuclear weapons mounted during the 1960s, arms-control negotiations between the United States and the Soviet Union began to produce agreements. In 1963 the two major nuclear powers accepted the Limited Test Ban Treaty, committing themselves

> to prohibit, to prevent and not to carry out any nuclear weapon test explosion or any other nuclear explosion, at any place under its jurisdiction or control . . . in the atmosphere, beyond its limits, including outer space or underwater, including territorial waters or high seas. . . .[3]

After 1964, the year in which The People's Republic of China detonated its first nuclear bomb, a new fear about nuclear weapons arose: the concern that many nations—of varying degrees of international responsibility—would acquire nuclear weapons. In 1968 the U.S., the U.S.S.R., and Great Britain signed the Nuclear Non-Proliferation Treaty, which prohibited assistance to produce nuclear weapons to countries not already possessing them. Two nations with nuclear capability—France and China—did not sign this treaty. Many nonnuclear nations did sign and agreed not to acquire such weapons.

In the late 1960s the Soviets and Americans met for a series of negotiations that came to be known as SALT—Strategic Arms Limitation Talks. By 1972 the two nations were ready to sign an important treaty designed to reduce the danger of the arms race. In a later review of the negotiations, the agreement was described as follows:

The 1972 treaties collectively known as SALT I consisted essentially of two agreements: (a) the Anti-Ballistic Missile (ABM) Treaty which indefinitely restricted to a small number the deployment by both sides of anti-ballistic missile systems (or anti-missile missiles); and (b) an Interim Agreement to freeze for five years the number of offensive strategic ballistic missile launchers to the number then deployed or under construction in each country.[4]

Following the SALT I agreement, a second round of U.S.-U.S.S.R. negotiations (SALT II) was begun; it continued from 1972 to 1979, when President Jimmy Carter and Chairman Leonid Brezhnev signed a new treaty that would have placed various restrictions on the numbers and kinds of nuclear warheads and launchers in each country's arsenal. The U.S. Senate failed to ratify the treaty, and this failure contributed to the new phase of moral concern over potential nuclear war.

In the decade 1965-75 the United States was embroiled in a war in Vietnam, a war that for all its bloodiness and destruction did not involve the use of nuclear weapons. That war spurred a renewed examination of the just-war philosophy, which in the 1950s and early 1960s had been studied for its implications for nuclear war. As more American citizens claimed moral principles for their opposition to the Vietnam war, just-war criteria came under popular scrutiny. Ironically, concern about nuclear war was less evident as concern about the Vietnam war rose and as it became clear that the U.S. had rejected use of nuclear arms. Much of the published writing of theologians and philosophers in the late 1960s and early 1970s took up such moral issues as counterinsurgency warfare, interference in a country such as Vietnam by a great power such as the U.S., and U.S. selective service. Although great international tensions persisted because of the war in Vietnam, an optimistic mood about U.S.-U.S.S.R. relations accompanied arms-control treaties being negotiated and signed.

During the same period Pope Paul VI, who headed the Roman Catholic Church from 1964 to 1978, spoke frequently

30 NO EASY ANSWERS

on the danger and morality of war and nuclear weapons. In 1965 he spoke to the United Nations General Assembly, using words quoted again and again in ensuing years, urging the diplomats to take "an oath which must change the future history of the world: No more war, war never again!" He strongly urged disarmament ("Let the weapons fall from your hands") but conceded that "defensive arrangements will, alas, be necessary" (Heyer, *Key Statements*, pp. 23-24).

A consistent theme in Paul VI's statements on war and nuclear arms was severe condemnation of the arms race. In his 1967 encyclical *On the Development of Peoples (Populorum Progressio)*, he denounced the arms race as "financially depleting" and "a scandalous and intolerable crime." In a World Day of Peace message in 1977 he called the arms race "a false and dangerous program" and alluded to "this senseless cold war resulting from the progressive increase of the military potential of the various nations" (ibid., pp. 25-26, 32).

Compared to restrained papal rhetoric of the past, Pope Paul VI's choice of words and phrases revealed his deep emotional response to the nuclear-arms issue and at the same time raised the temperature of the worldwide debate over the morality of war and of nuclear weapons. In 1972 the pope called the arms race "an epidemic phenomenon" and a "contagion." In 1976 he referred to the bombing of Hiroshima as "butchery of untold magnitude." In 1978 he denounced "the absurdity of modern war" and nuclear weapons as "the most fearsome menace with which mankind is burdened" (ibid., pp. 27, 30, 33, 40).

The current debate over the morality of nuclear armaments began with the dashed hopes for the SALT II treaty; with the emergence of a revitalized Republican party and its 1980 presidential candidate Ronald Reagan, who proposed greatly increased defense spending; with the reemergence of the production and planned deployment of the neutron bomb and the MX missile; and with newly increased dangers in Europe and plans to increase the nuclear defenses of that region by deploying newly developed Pershing and cruise missiles.

By 1980 the nuclear era was thirty-five years old. Great intellectual effort had been made to define the moral and immoral aspects of the new weapons; several arms-control treaties had been agreed to by the major nuclear powers; no nuclear weapon had been used in war since 1945. Yet the arms race had over that long period raised to dizzying heights both the size of nuclear arsenals and their accompanying risks. Out of this milieu emerges the worldwide debate now spreading from international councils to federal and state legislatures, to town halls and classrooms, and to the streets of Europe and the United States.

Discussion Questions

1. What is the distinction between counter-city and counter-force nuclear strategies? Is the distinction important in moral terms?
2. The Roman Catholic bishops at Vatican II urged that war in the modern world be evaluated "with an entirely new attitude." What new attitude might they have had in mind?
3. Can peace achieved by a "balance of terror" ever be morally acceptable?
4. The United States and the Soviet Union have reached agreements such as the Limited Test Ban Treaty and the Nuclear Non-Proliferation Treaty. Has this fact given hope that the arms race can be controlled by bilateral negotiation?
5. In 1965 Pope Paul VI urged United Nations diplomats to take the oath, "No more war, war never again!" What part might the U.N. play in ending war?

PART TWO

Moral Issues

3

NUCLEAR WAR

Counter-city and Counter-force

Our world lives with the knowledge that two powerful nations possess huge arsenals of nuclear-armed missiles capable of reaching each other in minutes and capable of destroying entire cities with a single explosion. The United States and the Soviet Union have arrived at a rough equality of nuclear war-making power—a parity of mutual destructive strength. But strategists and statesmen continue to dispute both how nuclear military strength is measured and which of the two superpowers is stronger. Most experts agree, however, that the U.S. and the U.S.S.R. could destroy each other many times over.

A full-scale counter-city nuclear war between these two countries would reduce a large part of the globe to utter devastation: death or injury to millions of people, vast material damage, an earth left uninhabitable for many years by radioactive contamination. This potential disaster—often called a holocaust—the worst mankind has ever been capable of, has generated the central moral issue of the modern age. Despite the horrible possibilities of a future nuclear war, the moral judgments called for raise disturbing complexities.

The immediate and long-range consequences of all-out nuclear war have merited unreserved condemnation by virtually all moral philosophers and theologians. Pope John Paul II, speaking in Hiroshima in 1981, recalled the atomic-bomb destruction of that city and said, "To remember Hiroshima is to abhor nuclear war" (Heyer, *Key Statements*, p. 53).

Contemporary weapons are much more powerful than the Hiroshima and Nagasaki bombs. Many scientific studies have

34

been carried out to estimate both the damage that would be caused by a single large nuclear bomb dropped on a modern city and the short- and long-range effects of multiple bombs exploded throughout a modern industrialized society. A particularly horrifying review of the worst possibilities of widespread nuclear war appears in *The Fate of the Earth* by Jonathan Schell. If the United States were subjected to a full-scale nuclear attack, Schell writes,

> . . . the vast majority of the people in the regions first targeted would be irradiated, crushed, or burned to death. . . . virtually all the habitations, places of work, and other man-made things there—substantially the whole human construct in the United States—would be vaporized, blasted, or otherwise pulverized out of existence. . . . fires would simply burn down the United States.[1]

Physicians for Social Responsibility, organized by professionals and students in health fields, has undertaken to provide information to the public about the effects of nuclear explosions. Howard Hiatt, dean of the Harvard School of Public Health, has written that "no effective medical response can be conceived to deal with the human damage that would result" from nuclear war.[2] Dr. Hiatt, drawing on research by the U.S. Arms Control and Disarmament Agency, describes the effects of a nuclear explosion over New York City of a bomb with the explosive power of one million tons of TNT (one megaton), detonated 6,500 feet above the Empire State Building.

> The area of total destruction, the circle within which even the most heavily reinforced concrete structures do not survive, has a radius of 1.5 miles. . . . Within this circle, almost all the population is killed.
>
> At a distance of three miles from the center of the blast, . . . heat from the explosion and the spontaneous ignition of clothing cause third-degree flash burns over much of the body, killing most people in this area.
>
> More than four miles from the center, brick and wood-frame buildings are destroyed, and fires caused by the

intense heat are fanned by 160-mile-per-hour winds.
. . . If we assume a population for the metropolitan
area of 16 million, more than 1,600,000 are killed. There
are 2,800,000 injured. . . . (Wallis, *Waging Peace*, pp.
82-83)

Soviet scientists have also contributed to the knowledge of
potential effects of modern nuclear war. A delegation from the
U.S.S.R. testified at the First International Conference of Physicians Against Nuclear War held in Washington, D.C., in
1981. Their report estimated the casualties probably to be
inflicted on a city of one million population by a one-megaton
bomb exploded in the air.

Killed   310,000
Injured   380,000
Uninjured   310,000
(A. A. Bayev, "Can There Be Life After Doomsday?"
Christianity and Crisis, 18 Jan. 1982, p. 379)

If such a bomb were exploded on the ground, somewhat
fewer direct casualties could be expected, according to this
report, but the resulting radioactive fallout would spread the
devastation over a much larger area.

In 1976, the Roman Catholic bishops of the United States
gave a moral response to the possibilities of large-scale nuclear
war: "With respect to nuclear weapons, at least those with
massive destructive capability, the first imperative is to prevent
their use" (*Catholic Mind*, Dec. 1979, p. 52). In 1979, Cardinal John J. Krol, testifying before the U.S. Senate Foreign
Relations Committee on behalf of the National Conference of
Catholic Bishops, said it is morally imperative that "innocent
lives . . . not [be] open to direct attack." He characterized this
proscription as "the central moral affirmation of the Christian
teaching on war" (ibid., p. 52). Krol also alluded to the traditional just-war philosophy, which includes the right of self-
defense for a nation: "The perspective which shapes this testimony, therefore, recognizes that some forms of war can be

morally legitimate, but judges that nuclear war surpasses the boundaries of legitimate self-defense" (ibid., p. 51).

This simple and direct condemnation of the use of strategic nuclear weapons—weapons designed to destroy entire cities— is not a condemnation unique to the nuclear age. Direct attacks upon innocent victims are always proscribed, Krol said. The principle invoked here implies, for some analysts, that use of some nonnuclear weapons in World War II was immoral and that the bombing of Hiroshima and Nagasaki cannot be morally justified.

In World War II, beginning in Europe and later extending to the War in the Pacific, many cities were partially or almost wholly destroyed by Axis and Allied bombing. Nazi Germany raided London—first with bombs dropped from airplanes, later with rockets, the precursors of today's missiles. In retaliation, British and American air forces bombed cities in Germany. Later, the United States subjected Tokyo to intensive bombing and finally destroyed Hiroshima and Nagasaki with the new weapons.

In the midst of the war and before the atomic bomb was publicly known, a trenchant moral analysis of these counter-city bombings, written by the Reverend John C. Ford, S.J., appeared in *Theological Studies*. The term Ford used for the bombings that were then wrecking large cities was "obliter-ation bombing," and he defined that kind of warfare:

> Obliteration bombing is the strategic bombing, by means of incendiaries and explosives, of industrial centers of population in which the target to be wiped out is not a definite factory, bridge, or similar object, but a large area of a whole city, comprising one-third to two-thirds of its whole built-up area, and including by design the resi-dential districts of workingmen and their families. ("The Morality of Obliteration Bombing," Sept. 1944, p. 267)

The appropriate moral principle in such a situation, ac-cording to Ford, is: "It is always intrinsically wrong to kill directly the innocent civilians of the enemy country" (p. 272).

But has the circle of combatants as opposed to noncombatants widened so much in modern warfare that urban workers and their families can legitimately be considered part of a country's war-making forces? Ford decided that despite the importance of factories and of the economy in general to a modern nation at war, many classes of citizens remain innocent of complicity in the conduct of war. Therefore, he concluded, it was still true that "the majority of civilians in a modern nation at war enjoy a natural-law right of immunity from violent repression. . . . The great majority, at least three-quarters in a country like the United States, have such a right" (p. 286).

A second question arising from obliteration bombing brings into the discussion a subtle principle of traditional morality, the principle of the double effect. One standard formulation of this principle is found in an ethics textbook widely used in Catholic colleges in the post-World War II years.

The *principle of double effect* says that it is morally allowable to perform an act that has a bad effect under the following conditions:
1. *The act to be done must be good in itself or at least indifferent. . . .*
2. *The good intended must not be obtained by means of the evil effect. . . .*
3. *The evil effect must not be intended for itself but only permitted. . . .*
4. *There must be a proportionately grave reason for permitting the evil effect. . . .*[3]

Application of this principle to obliteration bombing, Ford wrote, would include a claim that the intention of the bombing is the destruction of factories, communications, military installations, etc., all of which contribute to the enemy's war effort. Killing innocent civilians in the process would, therefore, be an unintended side effect, not the means of destroying the war machine. It would certainly be done for grave reasons. Ford argued that the Allied bombing of German cities was certainly intended to kill innocent civilians; he gave examples, including Cologne, Berlin, and Hamburg, where large parts of cities' residential areas were destroyed. These facts, he concluded, made it highly unlikely that the innocent victims were only an unintended side effect of the bombing of military and industrial targets.

Ford offered a second reason to infer that the deaths of innocent civilians were directly intended. He quoted an official publication of the U.S. Army Air Force, *Target: Germany*, which used these words to justify the city bombings:

> Bombs behind the fighting fronts may rob armies of their vital supplies and make war so terrible that civilian populations will refuse to support the armed forces in the field. . . . *The physical attrition of warfare is no longer limited to the fighting forces.*

Ford also says that the Royal Air Force of Great Britain allegedly had as a part of its mission "dispossessing the working population [and] breaking the morale of the people" (p. 294). This "professed objective of undermining morale" further convinced Ford that innocent civilians' rights were being violated by "direct intent" (p. 295).

Ford devoted little space to disputing the Allied leaders' argument that obliteration bombing of German cities was justified as retaliation for German anti-city bombing in Britain. Quoting Winston Churchill in 1941—"We will mete out to the Germans the measure and more than the measure that they have meted out to us"—Ford dismissed his sentiments as "revengeful." Of the general argument in favor of retaliation, Ford claimed it was equivalent to believing that "any procedure whatever, no matter how brutal, is moral and legitimate for us to adopt once the enemy adopts it" (p. 296).

Finally, Ford concluded that even if the intentions of the obliteration bombings were morally acceptable, there was still no cause grave enough to justify such warfare. Allied leaders had claimed—or hoped—that the bombing of Germany would shorten the war and ultimately save lives. Ford declared that this argument was speculative and did not clearly demonstrate military necessity. But less than a year after Ford's essay appeared, shortening the war and saving lives was the major argument in favor of using atomic bombs against Japan.

Whatever moral reasoning applies to conventional bombing of cities during World War II applies clearly to nuclear bombing of cities. A single conventional bomb can be aimed at a military target or at a civilian target, but a nuclear bomb—even a relatively small one—will destroy both kinds of target. Contemporary critics of the use of nuclear weapons therefore argue that nuclear bombs are by nature anti-civilian bombs and automatically fall under the moral condemnation applied to the obliteration bombing of World War II. Of course, not everyone agreed with Ford that there are no causes grave enough to justify bombing cities in wartime. As many as eighty-five percent of the American people approved of the atomic bombing of Hiroshima and Nagasaki, according to a national opinion poll conducted soon after the end of the war.

In a 1979 testimony to the Senate Foreign Relations Committee, Cardinal John Krol asserted that the "primary moral imperative of the nuclear age is to prevent any use of strategic nuclear weapons" (*Catholic Mind*, Dec. 1979, p. 51). He was careful to modify the term *nuclear weapons* with the adjective *strategic*. In military parlance, a "strategic" weapon is a long-range weapon such as an ICBM—and such missiles carry nuclear warheads so powerful that large industrial cities are the most likely targets. The other kind of weapon—not mentioned in Krol's "primary moral imperative"—is the tactical weapon, which by definition is designed for short-range use on a battlefield or in other limited warfare. The distinction between these two kinds of nuclear weapons is not always easily made.

Krol based his condemnation of strategic nuclear warfare on a statement from the Second Vatican Council's official *Pastoral Constitution on the Church in the Modern World:* "Any act of war aimed indiscriminately at the destruction of entire cities or of extensive areas along with their population is a crime against God and man himself. It merits unequivocal and unhesitating condemnation" (ibid., pp. 51-52).

More recent moral condemnation of nuclear warfare by Roman Catholic leaders does not insist on the strategic weapon/ tactical weapon distinction. Roger Mahony, Catholic bishop of Stockton, California, wrote in 1982: " . . . any use of nuclear weapons . . . is always morally—and gravely—a serious evil. No Catholic can ever support or cooperate with the planning or executing of policies to use . . . nuclear weapons even in a defensive posture" ("Becoming a Church of Peace Advocacy," *Christianity and Crisis*, 1 March 1982, p. 37).

Yet one can readily conceive of restricted military uses of tactical nuclear weapons—for example, a strike on a missile-launching site, the destruction of a naval fleet at sea, an attack on a nuclear facility that manufactures the enemy's nuclear weapons. Realistic hypotheses for the tactical use of nuclear weapons are a constant concern of the North Atlantic Treaty Organization (NATO), which is obligated to plan a defense against a possible invasion of western Europe by the Soviet-supported Warsaw Pact nations. Central to the planning relating to nuclear weapons is the question, Should NATO respond with tactical nuclear weapons to an invasion conducted with only conventional armaments? Bishop Mahony is of the opinion that "it is not morally permissible to use nuclear weapons to deter mere conventional warfare" (ibid., p. 40), and he evidently means to include tactical nuclear weapons in this prohibition. Mahony's reasons for this moral limitation are based on his understanding that the Roman Catholic Church tolerates the possession of nuclear weapons only for the purpose of deterring their use. Yet it must also be true that persons such as Bishop Mahony believe that nuclear weapons are by their very nature qualitatively different from conventional weapons. If one accepts this claim, then all moral objections to strategic nuclear weapons can be expanded to cover tactical nuclear weapons and nuclear explosives of any kind whatsoever. But if one does not accept the claim, then the morality of tactical nuclear weapons becomes a separate moral problem.

Another argument against tactical nuclear warfare stems from a judgment that any use of nuclear weapons, no matter how limited, will escalate into a full-scale nuclear conflict, which has no moral justification. In 1981, Anthony M. Pilla, Roman Catholic bishop of Cleveland, argued—without referring to the distinction between strategic and tactical weapons—that nuclear weapons do not meet any of the traditional just-war criteria. Bishop Pilla asked himself, "Can there be a 'limited' nuclear war?" He answered with a quotation from Pope John Paul II's 1981 address in Hiroshima, "War is Death":

> The total consequences of full-scale nuclear war are impossible to predict, but even if a mere fraction of the available weapons were to be used, one has to ask whether the inevitable escalation can be imagined and whether the very destruction of humanity is not a real possibility. (Heyer, *Key Statements*, p. 148)

There is a logical difficulty with Bishop Pilla's opinion that this papal quotation rules out the possibility of a limited nuclear war, since the pope was talking about a "fraction" of the weapons to be used in a full-scale nuclear war, obviously strategic weapons. There is no support in John Paul II's statement for the assumption that escalation would be inevitable.

In 1981, John R. Quinn, Roman Catholic archbishop of San Francisco, also condemned nuclear weapons as immoral—again without attention to the strategic-tactical distinction. "The effects of our defensive weapons are no longer fully predictable or within our control," Quinn said (ibid., p. 160). He evidently saw tactical nuclear weapons to be as difficult to control as strategic weapons and thus deserving the same condemnation without distinction.

Some persons believe that the United States and the Soviet Union possess so many nuclear arms that nuclear war is inevitable. Thus they are morally opposed to the production and continued possession of nuclear weapons of any size or type.

The Christian Church (Disciples of Christ) in its 1981 General Assembly passed a resolution concerning nuclear arms that characterized all nuclear weapons—the qualifications of strategic and tactical were not used—as "a daily threat to this Earth and all its inhabitants" (ibid., p. 248). This threat is said to arise from the fact that "informed scientists now believe nuclear war to be inevitable before this century ends" (ibid.).

No distinction between tactical and strategic arms was made in an Episcopal Church statement—issued by the Primates of the Anglican Communion in 1981—which said that "the very conditions of a just war themselves condemn the . . . use of nuclear weapons" (ibid., p. 254).

In 1978 the Presbyterian Church in the United States adopted a resolution condemning all nuclear weapons as "an increasing threat of utter destruction if ever used" (ibid., p. 259).

The National Conference of Catholic Bishops (NCCB), in its pastoral letter on war and peace, raised a series of questions about the morality of using tactical nuclear weapons:

> The issue at stake is the *real* as opposed to the *theoretical* possibility of a "limited nuclear exchange." . . . While not trying to adjudicate the technical debate, we are aware of it and wish to raise a series of questions which challenge the actual meaning of "limited" in this discussion.
> —Would leaders have sufficient information to know what is happening in a nuclear exchange? . . .
> —Would military commanders be able in the midst of the destruction and confusion of a nuclear exchange to maintain a policy of "discriminate targeting"? . . .
> —Would not the casualties, even in a war defined as limited by strategists, still run in the millions? (*Challenge*, pp. 15-16)

The bishops concluded that crossing the threshold from conventional warfare to use of tactical nuclear weapons is an unacceptable moral risk:

> To cross this divide is to enter a world where we have no experience of control, much testimony against its possibility and therefore no justification for submitting the

human community to this risk. (P. 16)

Yet the distinction between strategic and tactical nuclear weapons raises doubts whether an absolute moral condemnation of the use of nuclear weapons can be sustained. In harsh military reality, strategic weapons demand most attention, for it is the ICBMs with warheads measured in megatons that most threaten the world. Deterrence—the vexing moral question in greatest dispute—chiefly concerns strategic weapons.

Discussion Questions

1. What is the distinction between strategic and tactical nuclear weapons? Is the distinction morally important?
2. In light of the principle of double effect, could the bombing of an industrialized city ever be morally justified? If so, under what circumstances?
3. Does the counter-city bombing of World War II teach any lessons about the morality of using nuclear weapons in the future?
4. In 1941 Winston Churchill said, "We will mete out to the Germans the measure and more than the measure that they have meted out to us." Can this principle of retaliation in wartime be applied to the use of conventional weapons? of nuclear weapons?
5. Roger Mahony, a Roman Catholic bishop, wrote, "It is not morally permissible to use nuclear weapons to deter mere conventional warfare." Do you agree, or disagree? Why?

4

DETERRENCE

The Morality of Intention

No nuclear bomb has been used as a weapon of war since 1945. However, tensions among the United States, its allies, the Soviet Union, and its client states have risen and fallen over the years. Big-power rivalry and mutual enmity are always dangerous to the Western world, and at times to the entire world. The cold war, as the East-West struggle has been called since the 1940s, persists. Both the U.S. and the U.S.S.R. have developed nuclear weapons of increasing power, along with delivery systems of increasing accuracy. Neither has chosen war, although the war-making potential of the two nations makes a devastating war possible—some say, even probable.

Why then does the United States maintain its huge nuclear arsenal, if relationships have been relatively peaceful for four decades between the nation and its most dangerous adversary in the world? The answer given by U.S. defense officials is: The Soviet Union is governed by aggressive, power-hungry leadership; it seeks expansion of the territory it controls; and its goals include fomenting unrest in order to expand Soviet influence throughout the world. Historical evidence to support this conception of Soviet intentions abounds—from the post-World War II subjection of eastern European nations to the suppression of the 1956 Hungarian Revolution to the Cuban missile crisis of 1962 to the invasion of Afghanistan in 1979 to the threats against Poland today.

American nuclear-weapons policy deriving from this view of the Soviet government is called deterrence. This policy

asserts that the U.S. needs a nuclear arsenal to deter the Russians from:
- a nuclear attack or threat against the U.S. or any U.S. ally;
- an attack with Warsaw Pact forces on western Europe, even with conventional weapons;
- interference in the domestic affairs of countries where the Russians perceive themselves to have some interest;
- blackmail based on the threat of using nuclear weapons.

Deterrence as a strategic foreign policy is justified by its proponents as the only acceptable way out of a cruel dilemma imposed by the Soviet Union: the impossible choice between a morally unacceptable nuclear war or an equally unacceptable domination of the West by Communist totalitarianism. Defenders of American deterrence policy also argue that U.S. military strength, including its nuclear arsenal, can be credited with preserving the nuclear peace since World War II—no matter how shaky that peace has been.

Deterrence policy receives widespread public support. Michael Novak, a lay Catholic theologian, calls it "the plainly expressed will of the American people, who have chosen to preserve their institutions through deterring both nuclear war and totalitarian might."

Novak has spoken out clearly on the goals and achievements of American deterrence policy: "a moral, religious, and political good worth the sacrifice of one's life and energies, if anything in history has ever been" ("Arms and the Church," *Commentary*, March 1982, p. 41). Also defending deterrence on religious grounds is John P. Lehman, Jr., Secretary of the Navy in the Reagan administration, who identifies the armed defenses of the U.S. as "a firm reaffirmation of the great religious tradition that has always subtended our willingness to defend our Judeo-Christian Western values" (*Origins*, 1 April 1982, p. 674).

One of the editors of *The New Republic* has defended deterrence as a policy midway between unilateralism and the belief that the U.S. can fight and win a nuclear war. In a provocative article Leon Wieseltier writes:

> That is the most pressing reason for preserving the doctrine of deterrence—these missiles and warheads are not going away. If you do not believe that we should unilaterally disarm, and you do not believe that we should fight a war, and you do not believe that the arms race should forever be run, then you must believe in deterrence. ("The Great Nuclear Debate," *The New Republic*, 10 and 17 Jan. 1983, p. 36)

The preponderance of moral and religious commentary on deterrence in the 1980s, however, has asserted the immorality of U.S. deterrence policy, or has at least questioned its morality. The NCCB pastoral letter states, "There are moral limits to deterrence policy . . . Specifically, it is not morally acceptable to intend to kill the innocent as part of a strategy of deterring nuclear war" (*Challenge*, p. 17).

The two sides agree that if government policy is to have any moral status, its aim ought to be to prevent nuclear war. Critics of deterrence, however, charge the policy itself as immoral, even if it has prevented nuclear war.

In his 1979 testimony to the Senate Foreign Relations Committee, Cardinal John J. Krol not only condemned the use of strategic nuclear weapons but said, "The *declared intent* to use them involved in our deterrence policy is wrong." He seemed to imply that an intent to use is a part of U.S. deterrence policy and thus immoral. He went on to say, however, that "Catholic moral teaching is willing . . . to tolerate the possession of nuclear weapons for deterrence" as long as there is some hope of reducing nuclear armaments by international negotiations. This tolerance, Krol said, is "the lesser of two evils." Thus he appeared to have found deterrence to be an immoral policy but not as immoral as giving up the opportunity to negotiate the reduction of the great powers' nuclear weapons (*Catholic Mind*, Dec. 1979, p. 52).

The moral philosophy supporting Cardinal Krol's first assertion, that the "declared intent" to use strategic nuclear weapons is immoral, connects the evil action itself to the intention to commit the act. Thus, the argument goes, a person who plans to commit murder but who is prevented by some outside force from carrying out his plan is as morally guilty as if he had actually committed the murder.

When the argument is carried only this far, it raises several questions:

For example, is the intent of deterrence policy really analogous to the plan of a murderer? Or is the real intent of deterrence policy to prevent nuclear war, rather than to wage such a war? In other words, is the threat inherent in U.S. deterrence policy really the same threat as that of a robber demanding, "Your money or your life"?

Another question: Does the deployment of the U.S. deterrent force necessarily imply that this nation would indeed launch its strategic missiles when sufficiently provoked by the U.S.S.R., or can the deterrent force be held as a bluff—a bluff the Soviets will never be able to call?

The first of these questions, concerning the meaning of intent, has in the view of many contemporary religious thinkers an obvious answer. If deterrence is an immoral intention, then the U.S. must dismantle its nuclear arsenal or be justly denounced as a nation with an evil nuclear policy.

For others, including some Roman Catholic bishops in favor of disarmament and other peace initiatives, deterrence contains a serious ambiguity. According to Cardinal Humberto Medeiros, Roman Catholic archbishop of Boston, "In following a deterrence strategy, nations threaten and prepare to take actions which can have catastrophic effects upon life in this world. At the same time the intention which leads to such threats and preparations is the intention to prevent nuclear war" (Heyer, *Key Statements*, p. 238). To Cardinal Medeiros, the ambiguity in the meaning of deterrence implies that such a national policy can be a moral policy. The question to be answered, according to Medeiros, is factual: Does deterrence policy actually prevent war and lead to the more desirable goal of arms control?

The NCCB pastoral letter accepts preventing the actual initiation of a nuclear conflict as the purpose of deterrence. But it characterizes deterrence policy as a "moral and political paradox" (*Challenge*, p. 16), because the policy makes the prevention of war dependent on massive production and deployment of nuclear armaments.

In the NCCB statement, the bishops' moral judgment on deterrence follows an analysis made by Pope John Paul II in a message to the United Nations' Second Special Session on Disarmament in 1982. The pope's conclusion, which the bishops adopt as their own, is: "In current conditions 'deterrence' based on balance, certainly not as an end in itself but as a step on the way toward a progressive disarmament, may still be judged morally acceptable" (p. 17). The bishops appear reluctant in their moral approval of deterrence, for they characterize their position as "a strictly conditioned moral acceptance of deterrence" (p. 18). Deterrence is not, they insist, "adequate as a long-term basis for peace" (ibid.).

With this careful reasoning the Roman Catholic bishops of the United States appear to be seeking a middle ground in the wide spectrum of moral judgments on nuclear deterrence. If in fact U.S. defensive nuclear weapons do deter a Soviet attack, then those weapons ought to be deployed wherever and however the deterrence is the most effective. Still, how such weapons can be morally targeted remains a problem to be faced by thinkers such as the American Roman Catholic bishops.

A serious moral question arises from the bishops' carefully wrought argument on deterrence: whether one can condemn all uses of nuclear weapons and at the same time accept deterrence even in the conditional form expressed in John Paul II's speech to the U.N. In other words, if no nuclear weapons can be used morally and if the declared intent to use them is also morally impermissible, then how can a deterrent policy be morally acceptable?

Secretary of the Navy John P. Lehman, Jr., found nothing new in the bishops' analysis of the moral status of deterrence: "The threat to take human life in order to preserve it has always been a central dilemma: the nuclear era raises this dilemma to global proportions but does not change its essential moral significance" (*Wall Street Journal*, 16 Nov. 1982).

National Security Advisor William P. Clark, speaking on behalf of the Reagan administration, welcomed the bishops' defense of deterrence and pointed out that—consistent with the bishops' dictum—the administration's deterrence policy "is not an end in itself but a means to prevent war and preserve the values we cherish" (*New York Times*, 17 Nov. 1982).

Gordon Zahn, Roman Catholic pacifist leader, characterized the bishops' conditional acceptance of deterrence as an "unfortunate suggestion that it would somehow be permissible to tolerate an evil of our own intent in order to forestall a greater evil we might have to suffer" (Pax Christi mimeographed papers, 1982). Analyzing the second draft of the NCCB pastoral letter, Zahn recommended that in place of the term "conditional acceptance" the bishops use a term such as "deferred condemnation" in order to "put primary emphasis upon the moral unacceptability of the 'threat' and 'intent' which . . . are necessary to make deterrence credible" (ibid.).

Sidney Hook, a philosopher and senior fellow at the Hoover Institution, lashed out at the bishops' analysis of deterrence:

> The bishops' position is morally irresponsible because it sins against the cardinal virtue of prudence. For 37 years, deterrents have prevented a third world war. Every just war results in the death of innocents, which is evil. But to declare we will not resist or retaliate, and thereby provoke war, results in far greater evils. (*New York Times*, 26 Dec. 1982)

Both critics and supporters of the bishops' letter and of similar statements often question whether the bishops are moving beyond the role of moralists and religious leaders. William V. Shannon, newspaper columnist and a former ambassador, believes that the bishops have now "entered into the nightmare world of the nuclear strategists and the deterrence theorists" ("If Not Nuclear Deterrence, Then a Conventional One?,"

Commonweal, 13 Aug. 1982, p. 427).

But it would seem that anyone staking out the middle ground will be pulled into this "nightmare world" by the very demand that moral problems be thought through to their practical conclusions. Those committed irreversibly to one extreme or the other tend to forget the enormous complexity of morality and reality. Many believe that nuclear weapons are weapons like any others and that therefore if the Soviets attack, Americans should fire back with whatever is in their arsenal. This simplistic idea can lead to the wishful thinking that says "nuclear wars are winnable." Many others use theological or moral principles to deny the moral validity of all nuclear weapons and of deterrence of any sort, making moot the question of which nuclear policy is the more morally acceptable.

In the 1980s more and more persons have joined the antinuclear weapons movement—both the prevalence and the influence of this view seem to justify the designation *movement*—because of their Christian principles. The United Church of Christ, for example, in its General Synod 13 in 1981, issued a statement recommending, among other things, that "the development and use of nuclear and biochemical weapons be recognized as completely contrary to the Gospel of Jesus Christ" (Heyer, *Key Statements,* p. 269).

From this perspective, shared by many of today's religious leaders, it is virtually un-Christian even to consider the possibility that nuclear deterrence policy might be acceptable to a Christian. Such simplicity—though clearly based on the Gospels—reduces the moral debate over nuclear weapons to straightforward yes-or-no questions: Are you for nuclear weapons, or against them? Are you for peace, or war? Dialogue—the give-and-take necessary in the United States for public policy to be truly public—is rendered impossible.

More than any other element of American foreign policy, deterrence is the central question for a national dialogue. To discourage public debate about the most urgent and difficult moral problem facing human beings by simplistic pronouncements is to divorce politics and morality at the very time when the consequences could be most horrendous. The NCCB pastoral letter has entered into such dialogue and has been both praised and blamed for the effort. But the criticism, if continued constructively, will itself stimulate the moral dialogue needed to accompany the policy dialogue.

By the same token, conclusions in the realm of morality arrived at by religious leaders cannot be allowed to dictate U.S. policy. All Americans, whether religiously affiliated or not, whether guided by religious leaders or not, belong in the great debate over the dangers of nuclear weapons and nuclear-weapons policy.

Discussion Questions

1. What is the goal of the United States' policy of nuclear deterrence? Is the policy morally defensible?
2. Does the policy of nuclear deterrence include the actual intention to use nuclear weapons? Or is the policy based on the possibility of deceiving potential enemies?
3. According to Secretary of the Navy John P. Lehman, Jr., the dilemma of nuclear deterrence is contained in "the threat to take human life in order to preserve it." Can such a dilemma be resolved?
4. If just-war principles cannot justify a nuclear war, can a policy of nuclear deterrence still be morally acceptable?
5. How can deterrence policy and "steps toward a progressive disarmament" (words of Pope John Paul II) be combined?
6. Who can best judge the acceptability of nuclear deterrence policy? Moralists? Political thinkers? Some combination of the two?

5

DISARMAMENT

How to Call Off the Arms Race

The governments of the United States and the Soviet Union, each acting according to its understanding of its national interest, have built nuclear arsenals of mammoth proportions. Should these entire arsenals one day be fired, much of the earth itself could be destroyed, for this and succeeding generations. Responsible persons of all religious beliefs or ideological persuasions know the immense danger posed by these nuclear arms. Yet the arsenals continue to grow as the two superpowers strive for military balance or military advantage, and as technological advances lead to new weapons. Thus the world faces the intractable problem of what is now universally called the arms race.

The solution to the problem can be stated simply: universal disarmament. But the demand for disarmament is deceptively simple. The diplomatic and logistical complexities of disarmament plans and their complex moral and theological bases continue to divide religious and moral thinkers.

Awe at the sheer size of the problem hovers over the debate. The U.S. nuclear arsenal contains about 9,000 strategic warheads (including bombs) and 22,000 tactical nuclear warheads. Comparable Soviet figures are evidently about 7,000 and 15,000. Delivery systems for these bombs include missiles—based on land, at sea, and in airplanes—which can at the press of a button devastate their targets in a distant continent in less than half an hour.

The question before all concerned people is how to reduce the numbers of these frightening weapons or even how to

53

eliminate them from the world.

The simplest proposal is unilateral nuclear disarmament. For the United States this proposal calls for the federal government to eliminate all nuclear weapons as a matter of deliberate government policy. A variant of this idea calls for elimination of all strategic nuclear weapons. In both cases the argument is this: On moral principle our nation cannot maintain a nuclear force; all nuclear weapons, or at least all strategic weapons, are anathema.

Some opponents of nuclear weapons speak generally enough to imply unilateral disarmament without making the specific demand. Sister Mary Evelyn Jegen, S.N.D., the national coordinator of Pax Christi U.S.A., for example, has written that the conditions of justice for participating in a war "cannot be met in using nuclear weaponry, and therefore we cannot acquiesce in a balance of terror based on a threat to use these weapons" ("Christian Spirituality, Disarmament and Security," *New Catholic World,* March-April 1982, p. 87).

A decision for the U.S. (or for any other nuclear-armed country) to disarm unilaterally would defy the conventional view of national security. It would be in some way an act of faith in humanity, which might include the hope that the Soviet Union and other possible adversaries would also disarm their nuclear arsenals. According to Sister Jegen, we need to find our security "not in political or military might, but in the way of God revealed in Jesus" (ibid., p. 86).

One form of unilateral disarmament would be to disarm some portion of the American arsenal in order to encourage our adversaries to do likewise. Such a unilateral initiative, as it is often called, would be a strategy of peace, in contrast to strategies of war represented by the continual increase of armaments.

What would be the consequences of unilateral nuclear disarmament? A pessimistic view is that nuclear blackmail might force the United States to capitulate to any Soviet demand, or that the Soviets might even launch a nuclear attack to reduce our society to ruins. In answer to these awful possibilities, proponents of unilateral disarmament either deny the probability of such Soviet actions or else accept the consequences in the name of morality. It would be better, some argue, to act morally even if the Soviets take over or dominate our nation than to participate in an immoral nuclear war that would destroy us along with many of our enemies.

The second and more widely proposed answer to the question of armaments reduction is bilateral disarmament. The U.S. and the U.S.S.R. would agree as sovereign nations that the interests of both would be better served if the nuclear arsenals of both were reduced or eliminated. There is some precedent (cited in Chapter 2) for successful bilateral negotiations in the areas of nuclear weapons, including the SALT treaties, the Limited Test Ban Treaty, and the Nuclear Non-Proliferation Treaty.

Some arguments supporting bilateral disarmament are based on virtually the same principles that others use to propose unilateral disarmament. George F. Kennan, former American ambassador to the U.S.S.R. and Yugoslavia, says in support of proposed negotiations, "I am unable to see how the Christian community can conceive itself justified in supporting even the cultivation or deployment by our government of nuclear weapons, much less the use of them, or even the threat of such use" ("A Christian's View of the Arms Race," *Theology Today*, July 1982, p. 167).

Frequently such a firm statement of moral principle is followed by a similarly firm call for unilateral nuclear disarmament, the logic being that if the deployment of nuclear weapons cannot be morally justified, then we must not have such weapons, regardless of what others may do. Kennan, however, does not adopt this logic, but instead says: "I recognize . . . that it takes two to preserve the peace, just as it takes two to make a war." Of unilateral disarmament, Kennan suspects it could be "a mere spineless unilateral capitulation" (p. 168).

When Americans such as George Kennan recommend a negotiated nuclear disarmament, they are in effect speaking to government officials responsible for initiating and conducting bilateral negotiations. But it takes two to negotiate as well. Because the Soviet Union has its own arsenal of nuclear weapons, U.S.-Soviet negotiations are necessary if bilateral disarmament is the goal—no matter what our judgment of Soviet intentions. Former ambassador W. Averell Harriman has said that arms negotiations are "the only clear path to security and survival, and the only path whereon we may shape our future instead of abandoning ourselves before uncertain whims of fortune" (*New York Times*, 2 Jan. 1983).

Among religious or political activists, one little-used approach to the Soviet leaders is to speak to them directly. Billy Graham, the American evangelist, carried his Christian message to Moscow in 1982 when he spoke to a world conference entitled "Religious Workers for Saving the Sacred Gift of Life from Nuclear Catastrophe." From this platform, Graham aimed his remarks at "nations" and "leaders of our world," attempting to speak in the same language to Russian leaders as he would to American leaders. Placing himself in the middle ground—"I am not a pacifist, nor am I for unilateral disarmament"—Graham urged "the leaders of the world to take specific steps for meaningful negotiations leading to major arms reductions" (*Christianity Today*, 18 June 1982, pp. 21, 23).

Christian Billy Graham appealed to the officially atheist Soviet leaders by lifting the discussion to a plane where he believed the two adversaries could agree, "the sanctity of human life." For the sake of human life, Graham argued, "we need to turn from our political and ideological conflicts . . . and moderate them" (p. 20). Just as the U.S. and the U.S.S.R. united against Nazism in World War II despite our contrasting ideologies, Graham said, so once again we face a "common enemy, . . . the threat of impending nuclear destruction" (p. 23).

Graham's approach parallels that of Roman Catholic popes. Rather than denouncing atheism or Marxism or Soviet aggressions, recent popes, confronting the horrors of nuclear war or the dangers of nuclear weapons, have appealed to all nations regardless of their ideologies or degree of responsibility for international nuclear tensions.

In 1981, in an address in Hiroshima, Pope John Paul II appealed to "the heads of states and of government" and "those who hold political and economic power":

Let us pledge ourselves to peace through justice; let us take a solemn decision now, that war will never be tolerated or sought as a means of resolving differences; let us promise our fellow human beings that we will work untiringly for disarmament and the banishing of all nuclear weapons; let us replace violence and hate with confidence and caring. (Heyer, *Key Statements*, p. 54)

In 1965, Vatican Council II, in its *Pastoral Constitution on the Church in the Modern World*, had addressed "all men, especially government officials and military leaders," and said: "It is our clear duty . . . to strain every muscle in working for the time when all war can be completely outlawed by international consent" (ibid., pp. 19, 20).

One difficulty is that such appeals may not influence heads of states. In democratic countries, where public opinion is regularly surveyed, particular religious groups often organize to translate their convictions into political action. American government officials are therefore likely to consider seriously the words of popes, councils, and religious leaders. However, authoritarian governments, such as that of the Soviet Union, presumably pay less heed to expressions of public opinion.

Soviet leaders, however, certainly fear an outbreak of nuclear war as much as anyone. This is the obvious reason why the Soviets have been willing to negotiate various nuclear arms-control agreements in the past. They may see the need to rise above ideological and strategic differences with the West, as Billy Graham said in Moscow, for the sake of human life. Despite the differences between East and West in responding to public opinion, the leaders of both sides do listen in different degrees to appeals made to all.

A moral appeal to heads of state faces a second difficulty— the hard facts of national interest. The U.S. and the U.S.S.R.

are rival powers, distrustful of each other, fearful of each other's strength, each responsible for its own territory and population. Under these circumstances it is unlikely that these two nations jointly would, in John Paul II's words, "take a solemn vow that war will never be tolerated." Negotiations at some future time might lead to such an agreement, but the pope's words propose some coming together of Americans and Russians independently of their national interests. That is unlikely in the world of sovereign nations.

A third objection can be raised to joint appeals to American and Russian leaders: The two nations are not morally equal. Indeed they are equally in danger of suffering greatly from a nuclear war, but it can hardly be maintained that the two are equally ominous in international affairs or equally dangerous in their foreign policies. For religious leaders to ignore the difference in moral climate between the U.S. and the U.S.S.R. seems to suggest that they perceive no important difference or that the difference is irrelevant. But it seems unrealistic to ignore this important difference by hoping for disarmament without negotiations. Whatever force there is in Pope Paul VI's 1965 plea, "Let the weapons fall from your hands!" the only method of disarming two nations simultaneously is by international or bilateral agreement.

Failure of the SALT II treaty—it was not ratified by the U.S. Senate because of the Soviet invasion of Afghanistan— led to apprehension that arms-reduction talks between the United States and the Soviet Union would end. In 1981, the new administration of President Reagan insisted that the cause of peace would be better served by building up American armed strength than by such talks. The administration believed that the Soviets had gained a military advantage and therefore presented an even greater threat to the world than heretofore. In this country the Reagan administration's plan to increase U.S. arsenals, both conventional and nuclear, aroused fears of nuclear war.

President Reagan, however, announced a proposal in 1982 for a new round of strategic-arms negotiations, to be named

START, for Strategic Arms Reduction Talks. In the words of Jan M. Lodal, a former senior staff member of the National Security Council, the proposal provides

that both sides reduce the number of warneads on their long-range missiles by one-third—from about 7,500 each to 5,000 each, with land-based missiles carrying no more than 2,500 warheads. In making this warhead reduction, each side would be required to reduce its total number of land and sea-based missiles to no more than 850. The United States also proposed phase-two reductions in which missile throw-weight—the missile's capacity to lift material into space—would be cut to a level below the present U.S. throw-weight level. ("Finishing START," *Foreign Policy,* Fall 1982, p. 66)

Preliminary START talks with Soviet diplomats began in Geneva late in 1982.

At the same time, a competing idea was rapidly gaining public approval—the idea of a nuclear freeze. The freeze proposal was first advanced in a 1980 document entitled "Call to Halt the Nuclear Arms Race," written by Randall Forsberg, director of the Institute for Defense and Disarmament Studies. Forsberg described the freeze as an "idea . . . to stop the nuclear arms race quite literally, by stopping the development and production of all nuclear-weapons systems" (*Scientific American,* Nov. 1982, p. 52) in the United States and the Soviet Union. The proposal's very simplicity contributed to its popular appeal. The freeze idea quickly received endorsements from many segments of society, in America and in Europe, even from the late Soviet leader Leonid Brezhnev. President Reagan also endorsed the idea but subsequently announced that the START talks should have priority until the United States was in a stronger negotiating position vis-à-vis the Soviets. The president also announced that the U.S. ought not to agree to a freeze until our nation had reached parity with the U.S.S.R. in nuclear strength.

As the basic concept of a freeze was further defined, differences emerged among those who endorsed the idea. Several competing freeze resolutions were introduced in Congress in 1982, principally one cosponsored by Senators Edward Kennedy, Democrat of Massachusetts, and Mark Hatfield, Republican of Oregon. The Kennedy-Hatfield freeze stated its objective: "The U.S. and U.S.S.R. are to decide when and how to achieve a mutual and verifiable freeze on the testing, production, and further deployment of nuclear warheads, missiles, and other delivery systems."

Verification of a ban on production of nuclear weapons would be very difficult, and the freeze resolution ran into opposition on this and other grounds. No vote on the Kennedy-Hatfield resolution was taken in the Senate in 1982.

In the House of Representatives, a freeze resolution introduced by Rep. Clement Zablocki, Democrat of Wisconsin, cleared the Foreign Affairs Committee but lost on the floor in August 1982 by an extremely close vote, 202-204. The Reagan administration opposed the resolution and offered a substitute resolution to endorse the START talks instead.

The idea of a nuclear freeze subsequently gathered support from many leading critics of nuclear armaments. In June 1982 backers of the freeze gathered in a New York City rally, the largest in the nation's history. A 1982 national poll by Louis Harris revealed that 73 percent of the respondents favored a ban by both superpowers on the production, storage, and use of nuclear weapons. Freeze resolutions appeared on the ballot in eight states, the District of Columbia, and numerous cities and counties and won approval in a large majority of cases. Organizations to direct the freeze campaign appeared all across the country.

Many religious leaders and other moralists endorsed the freeze. The National Council of Churches' Governing Board adopted a freeze resolution in 1981 that urged both the United States and the Soviet Union to "halt the nuclear arms race now by adopting promptly a mutual freeze on all further testing, production, and deployment of weapons and aircraft designed primarily to deliver nuclear weapons."[1] Also in 1981, the Unitarian Universalist Association's General Assembly called upon "the President of the United States to propose to the Soviet Union a mutual nuclear weapons moratorium immediately halting the testing, production, and deployment of all nuclear warheads, missiles, and delivery systems" (Donaghy, *Peace*, p. 37). Archbishop John R. Quinn of the Roman Catholic diocese of San Francisco in the same year called a nuclear freeze "a first realistic step toward a process of bilateral disarmament" and urged his hearers to give "active cooperation with other religious and community groups in this campaign" (Heyer, *Key Statements*, p. 163). In October of 1981, twenty-nine American Roman Catholic bishops endorsed "an arms freeze" as part of a statement condemning nuclear weapons as immoral (ibid., p. 182).

In 1983 the Roman Catholic bishops' pastoral letter *The Challenge of Peace* urged "immediate, bilateral, verifiable agreements to halt the testing, production and deployment of new nuclear weapons systems" (*Challenge*, p. 18).

In the spring of 1983, the U.S. House of Representatives renewed its debate on a nuclear weapons-freeze resolution. By a vote of 278 to 149 on May 4, the House adopted a freeze resolution calling for U.S.-U.S.S.R. negotiations to aim at both "an immediate, mutual and verifiable freeze" and "immediate, mutual and verifiable reductions in nuclear weapons."

The nuclear freeze appears to be an idea that can unite many persons whose moral stances on nuclear weapons differ significantly. Those advocating that the freeze be unilateral remain a separate group, but even they join in efforts to convince the Congress and the administration to adopt resolutions leading to a bilateral freeze.

Discussion Questions

1. Are nuclear weapons so dangerous that the United States, despite its ideological and political differences with the Soviet Union, should search for ways to reduce its nuclear arsenal?
2. If the United States were to disarm its nuclear force and retain its conventional military force, what dangers—if any—from the Soviet Union would the U.S. face?
3. Can American public opinion influence our government's willingness to negotiate disarmament treaties with the Soviet Union? If so, how? Can American public opinion help to persuade the U.S.S.R. to negotiate with the U.S.? If so, how?
4. Some people believe that if the United States builds up its nuclear arsenal, the Soviets will be more likely to negotiate arms reductions. Do you agree? Why?
5. If the United States were to freeze the production of nuclear weapons unilaterally, do you think the Soviet Union would follow suit?
6. What makes the idea of a bilateral nuclear freeze so widely appealing? All things considered, do you favor the freeze?

6

POSSESSION OF NUCLEAR
WEAPONS

Tolerable, or Not?

The Intercommunity Center for Peace and Justice circulated a petition among American Roman Catholic bishops in 1981. One bishop, Raymond Lucker of New Ulm, Minnesota, paused over one stark declaration: "The possession of nuclear weapons is immoral." Later, Bishop Lucker said that he then experienced a kind of conversion, that for the first time he fully realized the deep moral evil of the nuclear arms race and of the nuclear arsenal of his own nation. He signed the petition and became one more religious leader opposed to the nuclear-weapons policy of the United States—opposed to the weapons themselves on the grounds of moral principle.

The petition condemned even limited nuclear war, asserted that "the arms race robs the poor," and supported a nuclear-arms freeze and a cut in the U.S. military budget. Twenty-nine Roman Catholic bishops signed it. The petition gave as its source "our faith vision and our mounting concern over the increased probability of nuclear war" (Heyer, *Key Statements,* p. 182).

Moral disapproval of the possession of nuclear arms starts from a moral condemnation of anti-civilian, counter-city nuclear war. From this generally accepted principle proponents derive a moral condemnation of limited nuclear war; they argue that no nuclear war will remain limited once begun. Thus, to approve of nuclear war limited to morally acceptable military targets would be tantamount to approving inevitable escalation to an all-out war that cannot be morally justified. Blanket condemnation of all nuclear combat leads next to the proposition that an intention to wage nuclear war is itself immoral, since an intention to perform an evil act is also evil.

At this point in the logical chain one must consider the actual nuclear arsenal possessed by the United States. This arsenal is intended primarily to deter potential aggression by the Soviet Union, the other major nuclear power in the world. American missiles are aimed at Soviet targets; Soviet missiles are aimed at American targets. If the U.S. policy of deterrence is indeed equivalent to an intention to wage immoral war upon the U.S.S.R., then perhaps it logically follows that the very ownership, the very possession of these nuclear weapons is also immoral. This is the proposition that Bishop Lucker and twenty-eight other Roman Catholic bishops found compelling enough to endorse in 1981.

In his 1979 testimony on SALT II, Cardinal John Krol expressed the conviction that it is of the "utmost importance that negotiations proceed to meaningful and continuing reductions in nuclear stockpiles" (ibid., p. 104). If such negotiations continue to offer hope for a slowing down of the arms race, then "Catholic moral teaching is willing, while negotiations proceed, to tolerate the possession of nuclear weapons for deterrence as the lesser of two evils" (ibid.), the greater evil being the actual use of nuclear weapons.

The central moral concept in Krol's analysis is toleration, which is less than moral approval but more than being resigned to the existence of evil. The link he made between tolerating the possession of nuclear weapons and conducting arms-reduction negotiations leaves open the question whether deterrence would become morally intolerable if negotiations should break down.

Roger Mahony, Roman Catholic bishop of Stockton, California, also placed the notion of toleration at the center of an analysis of possession of nuclear armaments. Writing in early 1982, Mahony condemned all uses of nuclear weapons and any intention to use them as "always morally—and gravely— a serious evil" ("Becoming a Church of Peace Advocacy,"

Christianity and Crisis, 1 March 1982, p. 37). But he acknowledged that "many Christian moralists have held that the possession of nuclear weapons as a deterrent . . . is morally permissible" (p. 38). Claiming that current U.S. deterrent policies do not meet the demands of morality, Mahony argued:

The only possible Catholic support for a national nuclear-deterrence policy depends on three related moral judgments:

First, that the primary moral imperative is to prevent any use of nuclear weapons under any circumstances;

Second, that the possession of nuclear weapons is always an evil which could at best be tolerated, but only if the deterrence strategy is used in order to make progress on arms limitation and reduction;

Third, that the ultimate goal of what remains at best an interim deterrence policy is the eventual elimination of nuclear arms and of the threat of mutual assured destruction. (Ibid.)

For Bishop Mahony, employing the concept of toleration constitutes a "nuanced but tenuous Catholic argument for a limited and interim nuclear deterrence policy" (p. 41).

The NCCB Committee on War and Peace, in its first draft of a pastoral letter on nuclear weapons—issued in June 1982—followed the argumentation of Cardinal Krol and Bishop Mahony, rather than leaving the matter, as the twenty-nine bishops did, with a statement on the immorality of possessing nuclear arms. Although the first draft did not condemn all possible uses of nuclear weapons, it did raise this hypothetical question: "If we were to reject any conceivable use of nuclear weapons, we would face the very difficult question whether it is permissible even to continue to possess nuclear weapons."[1]

Like Bishop Mahony, the bishops in their first draft said that "according to Catholic moral principles" they felt obliged to disapprove of the "deterrent that is in place" (NCCB, *God's Hope,* p. 33). Yet they found "honest disagreement" to be possible concerning the peacekeeping effect of a nuclear deterrent force. This placed the bishops' committee in a dilemma: how to question America's nuclear deterrence policy and at the same time approve a restricted nuclear deterrent. Attempting to resolve the dilemma, the bishops turned to the notion of "toleration of moral evil as that applies to the problem of deterrence" (ibid.).

What does toleration mean in this instance? The bishops might have decided that the present deterrent would be tolerable because there was no better way to protect the nation against potential Soviet aggression. Or they might have decided that since U.S. nuclear missiles are targeted against Soviet forces rather than against cities, the deterrent in place is within the limits of moral acceptability. But they took neither of these approaches. Instead, they chose in this first draft to rest their case on the concept of toleration, as did Cardinal Krol and Bishop Mahony.

The bishops' committee carefully explained how they intended to use the term *toleration*. First, they said, it must be recognized that "the deterrence relationship which prevails between the United States, the Soviet Union and other powers is objectively a sinful situation because of the threats implied in it and the consequences it has in the world. Yet movement out of this objectively evil situation must be controlled. . . ." (ibid., p. 35). Next, they said, being in an "objectively sinful situation" from which we cannot escape without unacceptable risks implies that we must tolerate possession of the U.S. deterrent. Whether toleration here is less than moral approval is a fine point of moral philosophy. As long as the Soviet Union continues its present course, it is likely that, as the bishops' first draft said, "unilateral withdrawal from this reliance [on deterrence] has its obvious and grave risks" (p. 37). Whether or not arms-reduction talks can be *successfully* pursued—as distinguished from simply being pursued—these grave risks would appear to continue to justify the moral toleration temporarily accepted by the bishops' committee.

The bishops' committee, however, altered significantly its analysis of nuclear deterrence in the final version of the NCCB pastoral letter. The concept of toleration was removed from the argument. In its place, the pastoral letter incorporated a term from a message of Pope John Paul II to the United Nations, delivered in June 1982, after the pastoral's first draft had been completed. John Paul judged deterrence "morally acceptable" if it is "a step on the way toward a progressive disarmament." The bishops' own view in the final version of their letter is virtually identical to John Paul's, but their judgment of deterrence as morally acceptable is stated with several qualifications. Instead of simply using the term "acceptance," they use "lack of unequivocal condemnation" (*Challenge*, p. 19) and the phrase "strictly conditioned moral acceptance of deterrence" (p. 18) to characterize their position.

Having accepted the current need for nuclear deterrence and having found it morally acceptable under specific conditions, the bishops implicitly approve the possession of nuclear weapons. They explicitly "do not advocate a policy of unilateral disarmament" (p. 20).

During 1981 and 1982 some individual Roman Catholic bishops spoke of the possession of nuclear weapons as a much less subtle and complex moral question. Bishop Leroy Matthiesen of Amarillo, Texas, became prominent for his declaration that possession of nuclear weapons is immoral absolutely. Amarillo is the site of the Pantex plant, which manufactures nuclear explosives. Bishop Matthiesen not only signed the 1981 Intercommunity Center for Peace and Justice's petition declaring possession of nuclear weapons immoral but told the employees of Pantex: "We urge individuals involved in the production and stockpiling of nuclear bombs to consider what they are doing, to resign from such activities and to seek employment in peaceful pursuits" (Heyer, *Key Statements*, p. 156).

Bishop Matthiesen was confident that his view would prevail among his fellow Roman Catholic bishops. In a *Life* magazine article in the summer of 1982—before the first draft of the NCCB statement had come out—he predicted that the NCCB would "vote to condemn not only the first use of nuclear weapons but the mere possession of them" ("The Bishop at Ground Zero," July 1982, p. 66).

This bishop's approach to the possession issue reveals logic that would lead beyond condemning the possession of nuclear weapons. By recommending that Pantex employees "seek employment in peaceful pursuits," Matthiesen was arguing that the immorality of possessing nuclear weapons implies that Americans cannot morally participate in their manufacture and storage. This logic implies even more about Americans serving in the armed forces, which are responsible for deploying and possibly firing nuclear weapons. (This subject will be taken up in Chapter 7.)

Bishop Matthiesen also perceived the political consequences of a moral stand against the very possession of nuclear weapons. In his *Life* magazine interview, after predicting that the NCCB would follow his lead in condemning possession of nuclear weapons, he further predicted: "The Catholic Church is on a direct collision course with the United States government, and I'll be right out there taking the brunt of it" (ibid.).

As it turned out, Bishop Matthiesen was wrong about the collective will of the American Roman Catholic bishops, so his expectation of a "collision course" will not be tested, at least not now. Yet the logic is compelling. For those who are sympathetic to Bishop Matthiesen's opinions, such a collision would be welcomed as a forcible public expression of a deep moral conviction, although what form that collision would take cannot be readily defined. Those concerned with the nation's political stability would view with alarm the potential for a collision—in any form—between fifty million American Catholics and their government and would believe that the logic leading to that end must be flawed somewhere along the line.

Other religious thinkers and religious organizations have condemned the possession of nuclear weapons. A 1981 coalition of religious organizations devoted to the cause of peace wrote and published a document entitled "The New Abolitionist Covenant." Use of the word *abolitionist* was calculated to remind readers of the abolitionist movement against slavery in the nineteenth century. Five organizations representing

Christians with roots in many different denominations issued this Covenant: The Fellowship of Reconciliation, New Call to Peacemaking, Pax Christi U.S.A., Sojourners, and World Peacemakers. Their purpose was "to place before the churches the abolition of nuclear weapons as an urgent matter of faith."

Comparing the problem of nuclear weapons to the problem of slavery, the Covenant said: "Christian acceptance of nuclear weapons has brought us also to a crisis of faith. The nuclear threat . . . is a question that challenges our worship of God and our commitment to Jesus Christ."

Making the judgment that the possession of nuclear weapons is immoral can have direct personal consequences. For example, if Bishop Matthiesen's suggestion that nuclear weapons assembly plant employees seek other jobs were to be followed, those employees would be required to make serious personal adjustments. To take another example, notice this formulation of "The New Abolitionist Covenant": "The building and threatened use of nuclear weapons is a sin—against God, God's creatures, and God's creation." For one who accepts that statement, it would be a sin to be involved in the manufacture of such weapons or in government policies to deploy them.

This approach to the possession of nuclear weapons had been expressed earlier in a 1976 article by Richard T. McSorley, S.J., entitled "It's a Sin to Build a Nuclear Weapon" (*U.S. Catholic*, Oct. 1976). The existence of nuclear weapons, Father McSorley wrote, cannot be reconciled with the Gospel injunction "Love your enemies." McSorley was still more direct: "I do not believe God approves of . . . the possession of nuclear weapons" (p. 12).

McSorley's ascription of sinfulness to the building of nuclear weapons struck a responsive chord in the Roman Catholic archbishop of Seattle, Raymond Hunthausen. Speaking in 1981 to a convention of the Pacific Northwest Synod of the Lutheran Church in America, Archbishop Hunthausen called our possession of nuclear weapons "the demonic in [our] midst." What challenged Hunthausen to oppose nuclear weapons in

this way had been, he said, Father McSorley's article. Hunthausen recommended unilateral disarmament as "one obvious
meaning of the cross" and concluded, "We must dismantle
our weapons of terror and place our reliance on God" (*Origins,*
2 July 1981, p. 111). Although Hunthausen had been shocked
by the use of atomic bombs at Hiroshima and Nagasaki, he
expressed his sorrow that he had not spoken out against nuclear
arms until many years after World War II. (He later expressed
his determination to withhold a portion of his federal income
tax as a protest against U.S. nuclear defense policies; this
subject is treated in Chapter 9.)

Michael Novak, a lay Catholic theologian, has often been
critical of those who condemn the possession of nuclear weapons as immoral. He argues that since "the situation is one in
which nuclear weapons now exist with very little likelihood
that they will ever . . . cease to exist," the real moral problem
is not possession of the weapons but rather "how to prevent
such weapons from ever being used" ("Nuclear Morality,"
America, 26 June-3 July 1982, p. 6). While some persons
believe that all nuclear weapons can some day be destroyed,
Novak believes that nuclear weapons are not likely to go out
of existence.

Novak's central argument is that the deployment of weapons
is intended to accomplish what both he and his opponents agree
to be the ultimate goal—prevention of nuclear war. Novak
argues for a deterrent:

> In order to deter the Soviet Union from employing its
> nuclear delivery systems either for military use or for
> political use, it is not sufficient for the United States or
> its allies to *possess* nuclear weapons. . . . a deterrent
> system must be reasoned and thorough; . . . it must be
> intentional; it must be the product of intelligence, fore-
> sight and will. (Ibid., pp. 6-7)

At this point in Novak's moral defense of deterrence—the
need not only to possess but to deploy nuclear weapons with
specific purposes in mind—a question arises: What moral basis

is there for deterrence policy? Novak argues that the moral worth of the U.S. nuclear deterrent force· lies in its purpose: "If the purpose of the system is to deter the use of nuclear weapons, the threat inherent in the system aims at a high and even indispensable moral purpose and does so in a morally sound way" (ibid., p. 8).

The difference between the positions represented by Michael Novak and by Bishop Matthiesen seems to come down to a difference about the intended purpose for possessing nuclear armaments. The pro-deterrent side finds the basic purpose to be the prevention of nuclear war—a high moral purpose. The anti-deterrent side finds the threat inherent in the deterrent to be immoral and thus finds possession of the weapons also to be immoral. The Roman Catholic bishops' pastoral letter on war and peace has attempted to bridge this gap in understanding by declaring nuclear weapons to be morally unsatisfactory for any conceivable use in warfare but morally acceptable for deterrence purposes.

Discussion Questions

1. If any wartime use of nuclear weapons is immoral, does it logically follow that the very possession of these weapons is also immoral?
2. Some persons believe that possessing nuclear arms is immoral. Does this belief require such persons to support unilateral disarmament for the United States?
3. If possessing nuclear weapons is immoral, should employees of a nuclear-weapons assembly plant resign from their jobs?
4. If possessing nuclear weapons is immoral, is it still permissible morally to support a policy of nuclear deterrence?
5. The New Abolitionist Covenant states that "Christian acceptance of nuclear weapons has brought us . . . to a crisis of faith." Do you agree, or disagree? Why?

7

MILITARY SERVICE

Is Peace Its Profession?

In 1947 the Congress abolished the Departments of War and of Navy and unified the American armed forces in a single department, later named the Department of Defense. The new name indicates a significant self-understanding of modern America's army, navy, and air force: The United States considers its military services to be essentially defensive forces—not organized for aggression or to start wars but to prevent them. The U.S. Army War College motto reads, "Not to promote war, but to preserve peace." The Strategic Air Command, whose mission is to deliver nuclear weapons to remote targets, has adopted the slogan "Peace is our profession."

To some members of the contemporary movement against American possession of nuclear arms, for the military to claim that its profession is peace is nonsense or patent dishonesty. Certain voices in the peace movement are often heard saying that the United States has become a militaristic society and that U.S. armed forces are preparing to fight a war rather than to defend the peace. At the same time, military leaders and many political leaders tell the military that its performance is crucial to the security of the nation.

In this climate of splintered opinion, all members of the military face grave moral questions: Is military service itself morally suspect? Has the civil society supporting the military changed from peace-loving to war-loving? Have nuclear weapons altered the moral status of the military? Should religious believers withdraw from or refuse to serve in those branches of the armed forces involved with nuclear weapons?

Military officers and enlisted personnel looking for answers to such questions have received advice from some religious leaders that implies that the nuclear component of military service is simply immoral. For example, Archbishop Hunthausen has characterized the Trident nuclear submarine base in his archdiocese as "the Auschwitz of Puget Sound" (*Origins*, 2 July 1981, p. 110). This grim comparison between a weapons system of the American armed forces and the mass murders of Jewish people by the Nazis was undoubtedly intended to dramatize his radical opposition to nuclear weapons. But the message received by American military personnel was different; to those serving at the Puget Sound Trident base or similar installations, his words implied that to serve in the United States nuclear-related services is hardly different from being a Nazi.

Thus American military personnel are virtually forced to consider the logical chain of reasoning reviewed in Chapter 6. That logic begins with the moral condemnation of counter-city nuclear warfare and can be extended all the way to a moral disapproval of the very possession of nuclear weapons. If one accepts that position, further reasoning can take the argument directly to the people who participate in manufacturing, testing, deploying, and using nuclear weapons. The question becomes one of judging the morality not only of weapons or policies but also of one's employment. The question is most acute in military service: May I morally serve in a military system that possesses nuclear weapons and is prepared to fire them under certain agreed-upon conditions? This question extends beyond the military to employees of the federal government who determine or implement U.S. deterrent policies.

The moral status of military service is a question much older than nuclear weapons. There have always been some people who could not reconcile their moral values with the military's usual requirement that one be prepared to kill fellow human beings. In contemporary America, conscientious objection has become a legally protected option for those whose religious beliefs forbid military service. Yet conscientious objectors have

been relatively few compared to the number of citizens who
accept military service.

Nuclear weapons have not changed that. Conscientious objection became more widespread than ever during the war in
Vietnam, but not specifically because of nuclear weapons. The
U.S. military service in the 1980s contains about the same
proportion of Christians of most denominations as the population at large—with the exception of small groups such as
Quakers, Mennonites, and Church of the Brethren, who as a
matter of specific principle refuse to serve.

What is new in the 1980s is not the composition of the
armed services but the public debate about the morality of
military service in a nuclear age. Often the questions are being
raised from outside the military itself. Religious leaders, including some Roman Catholic bishops, have offered moral
judgments strongly implying that a committed Christian ought
not to serve in the military, especially not in the nuclear forces.
None of these religious leaders, however, has yet made such
an implication explicit. Military persons are thus left to their
own knowledge and conscience to make difficult decisions not
demanded of ordinary citizens.

Some members of the military have chosen to respond to
the challenge of the peace movement with their own religious
and moral convictions. Secretary of the Navy John P. Lehman,
Jr., has called upon the "spirit of patriotism, a spirit that sees
no contradiction between serving God and serving in the defense of our nation in time of peace or war" (*Origins*, 1 April
1982, p. 673). In his judgment, military service is supported
by religious belief:

> I see no conflict between my duty and my religious be-
> liefs. To the contrary—my religious beliefs provide vital
> inspiration to my efforts. . . . We must demonstrate that
> our deepest and most profound religious beliefs and val-
> ues allow us to say—no, . . . they demand that we say—
> that we are determined to arm our nation so that freedom
> will not be crushed. (P 674)

Lehman's words expose the conflict between two understandings of the proper Christian attitude toward violence. According to one view, innocent persons and nations must be defended against unwarranted attacks, and violence is permissible and sometimes even morally required to accomplish this end. According to the other view, the pacifist position, Scripture and the Christian tradition condemn violence—both private violence and the potential violence connected with military duty.

In the nuclear age this dispute has taken on a new dimension. Assuming that military force in the pre-nuclear period would be morally justified for defensive purposes, can a Christian justify defending one's nation by deploying nuclear-armed missiles capable of killing millions of persons?

To Colonel Don Martin, Jr. (U.S. Army Reserve), a staff member of the Officers' Christian Fellowship, the question of the morality of nuclear-related military service is bound up with the purpose of the U.S. nuclear arsenal. "Our nuclear forces do not exist in a political-military vacuum," Colonel Martin has written. "We cannot discuss the morality of American nuclear forces without keeping that picture [of Soviet military threats] clearly before us" ("On Nuclear Deterrence," *Command* 30, no. 3 (1982):32). This argument applies to military service the same principles that support the morality of U.S. deterrence policy.

What is the alternative to serving in the nuclear military forces? Martin sees the alternative as accepting unilateral disarmament. But in his view, "unilateral disarmament seems to represent an abandonment of Christian moral responsibility and an action that would lead to the domination of the weak (if not the whole world) by totalitarianism" (p. 34). How, then, can nuclear deterrence be reconciled with the biblical injunction to trust in the Lord? Martin recommends: "Maintain strong military forces while trusting in God to help us use them wisely" (ibid.).

Military service in the United States is officially tied to
religious beliefs. In the "U.S. Fighting Man's Code of Conduct" appears the promise "I will trust in my God and in the
United States of America." All military personnel are required
to subscribe to this as well as to other articles of conduct.
Another very visible religious element in the military is the
chaplains' corps. Chaplains traditionally have not only held
religious services for military personnel but have also been
available to give advice on moral problems to those who ask
for it. In the nuclear age such problems obviously involve the
morality of nuclear weapons and of nuclear defense policy.

The Roman Catholic bishops' pastoral letter on nuclear arms
gives special attention to the moral problems of Catholics in
military service. (The letter's conclusions constitute guidelines
for the advice that Catholic chaplains might give.) Addressing
military persons with decision-making authority, the bishops
say:

> We feel . . . that we can urge you to do everything you
> can to assure that every peaceful alternative is exhausted
> before war is even remotely considered. In developing
> battle plans and weapons systems, we urge you to try to
> ensure that these are designed to reduce violence, de-
> struction, suffering and death to a minimum, keeping in
> mind especially non-combatants and other innocent per-
> sons. (*Challenge*, p. 28)

Evidently the bishops do *not* seriously question the morality
of military service in the nuclear age, though they apply traditional moral principles to the question of the planning and
execution of military actions. It would follow that the central
moral questions in the nuclear armaments debate are not special
concerns of military personnel. Only pacifists are saying that
military service itself has become morally unacceptable; others
who condemn the possession of nuclear weapons have not
claimed that military service is therefore not permissible. Those

with a moderate position—such as the Roman Catholic bishops—have not pressed any new moral demands upon the military. The central moral questions, in other words, seem to be those concerned with national policy and multilateral negotiations about nuclear weapons. With regard to such questions, all Americans have an equal concern, and civilian political leaders have even greater moral responsibility than military leaders.

This understanding seems to be shared by Major General Kermit D. Johnson, retired chief of chaplains of the U.S. Army. Although General Johnson disapproves of the "facile warmongering stereotype" that is "unfairly and uncharitably applied to the many fine leaders of our armed forces," in the 1980s he himself developed a new opposition to the potential use of nuclear weapons. Whereas he had earlier told the General Assembly of the United Presbyterian Church that it should affirm the just-war theory, he now asserted: "Nuclear warfare is indicted, not vindicated, by the limiting categories of just-war criteria such as due proportion, just means, just intentions and reasonable possibility of success" ("The Nuclear Reality: Beyond Niebuhr and the Just War," *The Christian Century,* 13 Oct. 1982, pp. 1014-15).

Johnson concluded as many civilian leaders have done. "The 'fact' of nuclear weapons has been superseded by a more compelling fact: that human beings have a right to life free of the risk of mutual nuclear annihilation" (p. 1017).

Military personnel sometimes picture themselves as living somewhat removed from ordinary civilian life, members of a special society devoted to the defense of the larger society. This view, largely romantic in the modern world, gives some credence to a belief that the military ought to be a special target of anti-war activities and criticism. But it would appear that military persons are no more—and no less—responsible for the moral status of nuclear armaments than are other citizens. A person may leave military service that has been deemed to possess immoral weaponry, and move across an imaginary line to civilian life. But this action cannot bring peace of mind. In

the nuclear age a person cannot escape moral responsibility
that readily, if at all.

Discussion Questions

1. Some people believe that because the United States possesses nuclear arms, every member of the armed services
   must evaluate his or her service in moral terms. Do you
   agree, or disagree? Why?
2. To whom can members of the armed services turn for moral
   guidance on questions about weapons of war?
3. Do the following persons have the same moral obligations:
   Someone in the U.S. armed services? An American political leader? A typical American citizen?
4. The code of conduct for the U.S. military includes the
   statement "I will trust in my God and in the United States
   of America." What is the exact meaning of this statement?
5. Is there a moral dilemma for the military forces as they try
   to preserve peace while preparing to fight wars?
6. If the United States were to engage in nuclear combat,
   would committed Christians be able to obey all orders to
   fire nuclear weapons? Which orders, if any, should they
   disobey?

PART THREE

Perspectives

8

PACIFISM AND NONVIOLENCE

Ideal, or Mandate?

Pacifism—condemnation of war and of all use of military force—has been part of Christian tradition from the early days. In the Roman Empire, during the first centuries of the Christian era, the small but growing sect that followed Christ's teachings lived according to beliefs that placed them outside organized society. According to a contemporary Norwegian Franciscan writer, Knut Willem Ruyter, "It would seem that the early church had in the beginning no intention of being part of, not to speak of changing, the order of this perishable world" ("Pacifism and Military Service in the Early Church," *Cross Currents*, Spring 1982, p. 56).

In the reign of Emperor Marcus Aurelius late in the second century, military service became an ethical problem for Christians. Most Christians refused conscription, and pacifism became the predominant Christian attitude. In the third century A.D. "The Church Order of Hippolytus" gave a mandate to Christians: "If a catechumen or a baptized Christian wants to become a soldier, he shall be excommunicated, because he has disdained God" (ibid., p. 57). Yet many Christians did serve in the army. The Order of Hippolytus was modified in the fourth century to permit obligatory military service, though it still forbade voluntary service.

The Old Testament, though abounding in stories of warfare, already taught the opposition to war that was to be greatly emphasized in the New Testament. The Old Testament ideal is written in the Book of Isaiah: "He will wield authority over the nations and adjudicate between many peoples; these will hammer their swords into ploughshares, their spears into sickles. Nation will not lift sword against nation, there will be no more training for war" (Isaiah 2:4, JB).

Peace is a recurring theme of the Gospels, spoken most powerfully by Christ in the Sermon on the Mount: "Happy the peacemakers: they shall be called sons of God" (Matthew 5:9). The spirit of Jesus' teaching is clearly a message of peace, including peace among nations. Although most early Christians embraced strict pacifism, the number who found military service compatible with their Christianity is evidence that the present moral dilemma has deep roots in Christian history.

Pacifism might have been more widely practiced if the Empire itself had not been converted to Christianity in the fourth century. Augustine of Hippo (d. 430)—and centuries later, Thomas Aquinas (d. 1274)—formulated moral principles governing the application of justice to war, both the justice of going to war (in Latin, *jus ad bellum*) and the justice of fighting in a war *(jus in bello)*. The contemporary theologian Richard P. McBrien has written, "The purpose of the just-war theory . . . was not to rationalize violence but to limit its scope and methods."[1] However, the claim that it was possible, though not probable, for a nation to wage a just war contradicted strict pacifist principles.

Over the centuries, pacifism has been an authentic Christian response to the fact of war, but not the only authentic Christian response. Emphases differed in different times, but pacifists remained much in the minority everywhere. Pope Pius XII, in his Christmas message of 1956, rejected pacifism as a legitimate option for Catholics. When legitimate democratic governments prepare armed defenses, Pius said, "a Catholic citizen may not make appeal to his own conscience as ground for refusing to give his services and to fulfill duties fixed by law" (*Theological Studies*, March 1959, p. 53). But in Pope John XXIII's 1963 encyclical *Pacem in Terris* (par. 127) some pacifists saw vindication of their beliefs in such passages as " . . . it is hardly possible to imagine that in the atomic era war could be used as an instrument of justice." Vatican Council

II brought to the modern Roman Catholic world a renewed
legitimation of pacifism in the *Pastoral Constitution on the
Church in the Modern World*, which explicitly praised "those
who renounce the use of violence in the vindication of their
rights and who resort to methods of defense which are otherwise available to weaker parties too . . ." (par. 78). Since
Vatican II, most Roman Catholics accept two valid choices—
pacifism and the just-war ethic.

Pacifism is a political philosophy. Closely related, but not
identical, is nonviolence—a broad individual and social philosophy. The commandments given by Moses in Deuteronomy
include "Thou shalt not kill," and to some Christians this
entirely settles the question of violence. In the Gospels, Jesus
seems not only to forbid violence but to require a nonviolent
response to violence. Jesus says in the Sermon on the Mount:
"You have learnt how it was said: *Eye for eye and tooth for
tooth*. But I say this to you: offer the wicked man no resistance.
On the contrary, if anyone hits you on the right cheek, offer
him the other as well" (Matthew 5:38-40).

Nonviolence as a rule of life has been a powerful idea in
Christian tradition, and some of its prominent exponents have
become heroes to many. One such person in modern America
was Dorothy Day (1897-1980), the co-founder of the Catholic
Worker movement in 1933. Nonviolence and pacifism were
two of her primary goals for herself and society, and she
effectively spread these ideas in the movement's newspaper,
The Catholic Worker.

Because believers in nonviolence have commonly been required to work against the opposition and sometimes the dis-
dain of large majorities as well as powerful governments, many
of them have developed courageous and persistent personali-
ties. Because of their courage and persistence they have often
been regarded as modern prophets or saints even when their
ideas have not been accepted. Dorothy Day was such a person;
her personal dedication to nonviolence and pacifism enhanced
the influence of her writings on social justice and world peace.

Because pacifists condemn all forms of warfare, both nuclear and conventional without distinction, acceptance of pacifism has been growing along with the fear that the human race now possesses weapons that can destroy civilization. Vatican Council II's praise of pacifism also gave the movement some legitimacy as a moral option. The Council's *Pastoral Constitution on the Church in the Modern World* offered what was interpreted as more wholehearted support of pacifism than the Roman Catholic Church had given previously. War, the bishops of Vatican II said, must be evaluated in our time with "an entirely new attitude." Although the Council did not define this new attitude, the phrase suggested a sharp turning point in the Roman Catholic Church's view of the morality of war and tempted pacifists to see in it an incipient acceptance of their position.

In the late 1960s and the 1970s, Roman Catholic and other Christian leaders and writers expanded and deepened their criticism of nuclear arms and especially of the accelerating arms race. Pacifists took this growing criticism as further vindication of their position. Bishop Thomas Gumbleton of Detroit, who has become a leader of Roman Catholic pacifists in the United States, wrote in 1980: " . . . it is unmistakably clear that it is no longer possible for a Catholic peacemaker to continue a quest for peace by seeking military solutions to any human problems, even those of injustice or oppression."[2]

When publicly expressed concern over nuclear weapons grew once again in the 1980s, pacifism won more converts. Pax Christi U.S.A., a Roman Catholic organization represented largely by pacifists and inclined to pacifist ideas, grew rapidly in membership; more than fifty American Roman Catholic bishops are listed as members. Public advocacy of pacifism also became more common.

Michael Kenny, Roman Catholic bishop of Juneau, Alaska, declared for pacifism in 1981. In a statement to his diocese, Bishop Kenny emphasized his belief in the ideals of the Constitution and the Declaration of Independence and acknowledged his responsibility to "preserve, protect and defend the

U.S. by word, by example, by force of reason and persuasion."
Nuclear weapons, however, Kenny said, turned him against
all war:

> But I will not fight for my country. I will not kill for this
> country. I am categorically opposed not only to the *use*
> but to the *possession* of nuclear weapons, because to
> possess them is to run the risk of using them; and there
> is no way on God's earth that we could ever justify the
> mass and indiscriminate slaughter of human life that would
> result.
>
> More and more I find myself in opposition to all mil-
> itary power. I *am becoming* what in common parlance is
> called a *pacifist*. (*National Catholic Reporter,* 6 Oct. 1981)

Bishop Kenny's logic makes clear how loathing nuclear war
and nuclear weapons may lead to rejection of war and of all
military force. Explaining the basis of his pacifism, the bishop
offers a biblical faith that has typically motivated Christian
pacifists:

> It is not political logic, it is not historical evidence that
> primarily move me. I am becoming a pacifist because I
> am striving to *learn of Jesus* who is "gentle and humble
> of heart." The more I learn of him, listen to his words
> and understand his life, the more clearly I see nonviolence
> as the only course for one who would be his follower.
> (Ibid.)

Although Bishop Kenny rejects political philosophy or history as a basis for pacifism, he opposes the political use of
weapons because Jesus used only "weapons . . . of the Spirit—
gentleness, patience, compassion, forgiveness, love" (ibid.).
He seems to claim that virtues such as compassion and love
not only are obligatory for true Christians but also can be
effective in establishing peace in the world. This argument has
not been effective in the world of international politics, but
pacifists continue to press their case in political terms.

Gordon C. Zahn, a sociologist and an influential Roman
Catholic pacifist, explains his political preference for pacifism

as a comparison of risks and concludes that pacifism reduces the risk of immoral behavior in war. In 1980, Zahn wrote:

I, as a pacifist, would prefer risking the evils we might have to endure as a result of too rigid an exclusion of war to the evils we would certainly be called upon to commit as the result of too easy an acceptance of actions deemed "necessary" by some military leader, thereby meeting the test of the "just" war. (Shannon, *War or Peace*, p. 236)

Zahn's argument turns the tables in the usual confrontation between pacifism and the just-war theory. Usually pacifists can win an argument in the abstract when debating other committed Christians, but just-war advocates often prevail in debates by insisting that nations must have the right to defend themselves against aggression. Zahn finds the opposite to be true. He claims that a just-war option opens the door to calling any military decision just and necessary. Therefore just-war criteria, he says, though defensible in the abstract, will not prevent immorality, and pacifist principles will be more effective against evildoing in the practical world of war.

The risk of pacifism, which Zahn prefers to the risk of irresponsible military decisions, needs to be carefully examined. If that risk includes policy decisions resulting in domination of the United States by an enemy such as the Soviet Union, then the risk may seem too great for any but committed pacifists. If, however, the risk can properly be called a risk for peace, then it may become attractive to nonpacifists as well.

Zahn clearly recognizes that if most Christians come to accept the pacifist approach to modern war, they may lose influence with their own government. He writes:

One possible objection is that adopting so "negative" a stance would remove or neutralize any influence Christianity and Christians might have upon "statecraft" and might even benefit the forces of evil and oppression in situations where the common good or a nation's survival might be at stake. (Ibid., p. 241)

To this powerful objection to pacifism in practice, Zahn offers two rejoinders: Spiritual salvation might in an extreme case require surrender to enemy aggression, and pacifists and others sympathetic to pacifism must work to ensure that the nation will not need to choose between surrender and committing immoral violence. The latter idea makes it possible for pacifists to participate in the policy decisions of a society that continues to possess a military force and to make military choices.

Pacifists may make a practical contribution to the defense of the nation by developing "nonviolent alternatives to war." Zahn himself suggests "means of defense" that would "permit believers [pacifists] to join the struggles for justice and oppose oppression without being obliged to injure or kill another human being" (ibid., p. 242).

An acknowledged advocate of nonviolent alternatives to war is Gene Sharp, a political scientist and sociologist. Sharp believes that since "mass conversions to pacifism are not going to occur" and since threats will continue to be a fact of our world, "new responses to the problem of war" must be developed.[3] Sharp recommends that aggression be resisted when necessary but without resort to military force. He cites examples of successful or partially successful resistances in recent history:

> German strikes and political non-cooperation to the 1920 Kapp *Putsch* against the Weimar Republic; German government-sponsored noncooperation in the Ruhr in 1923 to the French and Belgian occupation; major aspects of the Dutch anti-Nazi resistance, including several large strikes, 1940-1945; major aspects of the Danish resistance to the German occupation, including the 1944 Copenhagen general strike, 1940-1945; major parts of the Norwegian resistance to the Quisling regime and the occupation, 1940-1945; and the Czechoslovak resistance to the Soviet invasion and occupation, 1968-1969. (Ibid., p. 7)

Sharp recognizes that nonviolent resistance measures may be "irrelevant to the nuclear question." Yet in some aspects of U.S. nuclear-weapons policy, such as the defense of western Europe against a possible invasion by Warsaw Pact forces, nonviolent resistance may, Sharp argues, "constitute a more powerful deterrent and defense policy than can conventional military means" (pp. 11-12).

Pacifism in the nuclear age thus faces a dilemma of its own. Because nuclear weapons are more destructive than all weapons of the past, pacifists naturally wish to reject altogether nuclear weapons and the policies that permit their possession and deployment. But to reduce substantially the danger of nuclear war, pacifists need to work with U.S. policymakers on questions of nonviolent resistance to aggression. Should a pacifist, it must be asked, reject all cooperation with the military and the political structures that support it, and thus withdraw from political life? Or can a pacifist keep working to reduce danger of war and to develop nonviolent alternatives to war without compromising pacifist principles?

The American Roman Catholic bishops, in their pastoral letter, *The Challenge of Peace,* approached pacifism as one of the ways to defend peace. "The Christian," the bishops wrote, "has no choice but to defend peace, properly understood, against aggression. This is an inalienable obligation. It is the *how* of defending peace which offers moral options" (p. 8). The bishops recognize that "those who resist bearing arms and those who bear them" are exercising "two distinct moral responses" (ibid.). Both responses, they believe, "seek to serve the common good" (p. 9). But the bishops are careful to add that the moral options are "options open to individuals. . . . Governments threatened by armed, unjust aggression *must* defend their people. This includes defense by armed force if necessary as a last resort" (ibid.).

Pacifists and others who seek nonviolent solutions to national and international tensions believe more study and research might offer alternatives to violent or military solutions. A Commission on Proposals for the National Academy of

Peace and Conflict Resolution revived a longstanding idea in
1981 and recommended that a United States Academy of Peace
be established because "peace is a legitimate field of learning"
and because the Commission believed that such learning would
enhance the chances for real peace in the world.

Whatever complications pacifist theory presents, pacifist
principles clearly imply unilateral disarmament. Archbishop
Raymond Hunthausen put the case in straightforward terms:

> As followers of Christ, we need to take up our cross in
> the nuclear age. I believe that one obvious meaning of
> the cross is unilateral disarmament. Jesus' acceptance of
> the cross rather than the sword raised in his defense is
> the Gospel's statement of unilateral disarmament. We are
> called to follow. (*Origins*, 2 July 1981, p. 111)

And to the common demand that the United States must
protect its national security, Archbishop Hunthausen replies:
"Our security as people of faith lies not in demonic weapons
which threaten all life on earth. Our security is in a loving,
caring God. We must dismantle our weapons of terror and
place our reliance on God" (ibid.).

Discussion Questions

1. Many Christians in the early Christian era refused military
   service. Why? Does their position have any relevance today?
2. Has pacifism become more realistic in the nuclear era? Or
   is pacifism more dangerous in a world containing a totalitarian threat?
3. Pacifism and the just-war ethic, according to Vatican II,
   are valid options. But are these philosophies inconsistent
   with each other?
4. Does the commandment "Thou shalt not kill" apply to
   soldiers in wartime?

5. Can pacifists remain good American citizens when the nation is engaged in a war?
6. Are there possible nonviolent alternatives to nuclear deterrence?

9

NUCLEAR PACIFISM

A Practical Ideal?

Ever since the development of the hydrogen bomb in the late 1940s, most moralists and strategists have considered nuclear weapons to be qualitatively different from other weapons. The current debate over the morality of modern war continues to distinguish between nuclear war and so-called conventional war. This distinction allows some to propose that nuclear weapons be abolished and that the United States be urged to continue arming itself with only conventional weapons. Proponents of this policy think that nuclear weapons are immoral *per se*, but that using conventional weapons may be morally permissible. This moral position is often called nuclear pacifism; logically, it calls for unilateral nuclear disarmament.

Roman Catholic Archbishop Raymond Hunthausen speaks specifically about nuclear weapons, although he does not always distinguish them from conventional weapons. His arguments against nuclear weapons are similar to traditional arguments of pacifists against all military weapons and forces. He has called first-strike nuclear weapons "immoral and criminal" and has characterized nuclear weapons in general as "the demonic in [our] midst." On the basis of the Sermon on the Mount and Jesus' call to "take up [the] cross and follow me" (Mark 8:34), Hunthausen has strongly recommended unilateral disarming of the U.S. nuclear arsenal as "a moral imperative for followers of Christ" (*Origins*, 2 July 1981, pp. 110-11). Moreover, he took a step of active resistance to nuclear weapons in 1981:

> I think the teaching of Jesus tells us to render to a nuclear-armed Caesar what that Caesar deserves—tax resistance.

And to begin to render to God alone that complete trust which we now give through our tax dollars to a demonic form of power. Some would call what I am urging "civil disobedience." I prefer to see it as obedience to God. (Ibid., p. 112)

Early in 1982 Archbishop Hunthausen announced his decision to withhold fifty percent of his federal income-tax payments as his personal resistance to nuclear weapons.

Religious leaders who believe that the very possession of nuclear weapons is immoral do not necessarily state how their conviction might affect national policy. For example, Bishop Leroy Matthiesen of Amarillo, in his address recommending that employees of the Pantex nuclear weapons assembly plant seek other jobs, did not explicitly endorse unilateral nuclear disarmament. Yet the logic of opposing the manufacture of nuclear weapons inevitably leads to that position. Calling the military use of nuclear power "a vain hope for safety," Matthiesen said, "Let us stop this madness" (Heyer, *Key Statements*, p. 155).

Whether a particular call for the end of the arms race means unilateral disarmament or only negotiations with the Soviet Union is not always clear. For example, in 1981 the General Assembly of the Christian Church (Disciples of Christ) passed a "Resolution Concerning Nuclear Arms" that contained this language:

Be it resolved that the General Assembly . . . voice our deep conviction that this most heinous obscenity of the continuing nuclear armaments research, development, and production be brought to an immediate end; and we call upon the leaders of the nations to stop this madness and get on with those things that make for peace. (Ibid., p. 249)

The first part of the resolution reads like a recommendation for unilateral action on the part of the United States; yet the second part, referring to "nations" (note the plural), seems to suggest either international negotiations or some simultaneous decision on the part of all the nuclear-equipped nations.

Nuclear pacifism need not be related on the level of principle to general pacifism. The just-war theory—a set of principles rejected by traditional pacifists—can itself be used to justify total opposition to nuclear weapons. Some uncompromising opponents of nuclear weapons prefer to be identified as peacemakers rather than as nuclear pacifists. Bishop Walter Sullivan of the Roman Catholic diocese of Richmond, Virginia, has said, "I am not a pacifist but a peacemaker . . . but I have always opposed the just war theory" (*National Catholic Reporter*, 11 Dec. 1981). (The just-war theory and its relation to the nuclear-war question are reviewed in Chapter 10.)

Bishop Roger Mahony of the Catholic diocese of Stockton, California, uses the term nuclear pacifism, although his definition is new. In 1982, Bishop Mahony wrote in his article "Becoming a Church of Peace Advocacy":

> It is . . . important to recall that the moral reasoning involved in classic just-war theory led the bishops at the Second Vatican Council to declare that a form of nuclear pacifism is a weighty and unexceptional obligation of Christians. This means that any use of nuclear weapons, and by implication, any intention to use them, is always morally—and gravely—a serious evil. (*Christianity and Crisis*, 1 March 1982, p. 37)

What Bishop Mahony called a "form of nuclear pacifism" does not constitute an absolute rejection of nuclear weapons; in the same article, he argues that the deployment of nuclear arms as a deterrent is "an evil which could at best be tolerated" because deterrence might prevent the greater evil of nuclear war (p. 38).

The Netherlands Reformed Church has moved from a qualified approval of the possession of nuclear arms (a view similar to Bishop Mahony's) to a position more properly called nuclear pacifism. In 1962 the General Synod had condemned the use of nuclear weapons but had qualified that "No" with a "Yes"; in 1981 the synod explained, in a "Pastoral Letter to All Congregations":

The synod [in 1962] did not speak unambiguously about the possession of nuclear weapons. The reason for this was not because a qualifying clause was added to the "No" which implied a "Yes" to the deterrent function of nuclear weapons, but because "abolition" of these weapons was not possible in the normal sense of the word. . . . (*The Ecumenical Review*, July 1981, p. 250)

The synod's new pastoral letter went on to condemn the possession of all nuclear arms and to endorse unilateral nuclear disarmament:

. . . first of all, we must repeat our "No" of 1962 and then in all clarity state that this "No" also holds without qualification for the possession of all nuclear weapons. . . . Of course we continue to hope for steps toward bilateral and multilateral disarmament. . . . Since it has turned out to be impossible to reach multilateral decisions leading towards such steps, they should be taken unilaterally. (Pp. 250-51)

Although this synod called only for "the denuclearization of the Netherlands," the logic of its pastoral letter might be applied to the United States.

Unilateral nuclear disarmament in practice would admit of degrees of disarmament. One step would be for NATO to abandon nuclear weapons as part of its defense of western Europe and to strengthen its conventional forces. This strengthening would continue an effective military defense against the Soviet Union and the Warsaw Pact nations and allay fears that Europe might become the first nuclear battleground if the stalemate between the great powers ever broke down.

The U.S. Roman Catholic bishops' pastoral letter on war and peace raises moral objections to using nuclear weapons as a defense of western Europe against a conventional armed attack. The bishops state, " . . . we judge resort to nuclear weapons to counter a conventional attack to be morally unjustifiable" (*Challenge*, p. 15). They explain this judgment on the basis of probable escalation:

> The chances of keeping use limited seem remote, and the consequences of escalation to mass destruction would be appalling. Former public officials have testified that it is improbable that any nuclear war could actually be kept limited. Their testimony and the consequences involved in this problem lead us to conclude that the danger of escalation is so great that it would be morally unjustifiable to initiate nuclear war in any form. (Ibid.)

A moral objection to using nuclear weapons to defend western Europe implies that NATO's conventional forces must be built to withstand a potential Soviet-Warsaw Pact assault. The NCCB pastoral concedes this point:

> Rejection of some forms of nuclear deterrence could . . . conceivably require a willingness to pay higher costs to develop conventional forces. . . . It may well be that some strengthening of conventional defense would be a proportionate price to pay, if this will reduce the possibility of a nuclear war. We acknowledge this reluctantly. . . . (*Challenge*, p. 21)

The Catholic bishops' reasoning—from a risk of escalation to a prohibition of the first use of nuclear weapons in all circumstances—could also be employed to denounce retaliatory use of nuclear weapons against military targets. In other words, if risk of escalation morally prohibits the use of a weapon, no use of weapons creating the risk can be morally justified. The NCCB pastoral letter definitely objects to the first use of any nuclear weapons: " . . . in light of the probable effects of initiating nuclear war, we urge NATO to move rapidly toward the adoption of a 'no first use' policy, but doing so in tandem with development of an adequate alternative defense posture" (p. 15). Such a ban on first-strike policy may be sound, but it is debatable whether a first strike, even in retaliation for an attack with conventional arms, is morally prohibited as clearly as the bishops' letter claims. Risk of escalation is a judgment dependent on actual military planning and on the strategy and tactics that would be used in a limited war in western Europe. The risk of escalation cannot be said to be inherent in the weapons themselves.

Unilateral nuclear disarmament, whether carried out all at once or in stages, carries its own risks. If the nuclear arsenal deployed by the United States and its allies does in fact deter the Soviet Union and its allies from military or political aggression, removal of that arsenal increases the risk of aggression against the United States and its allies. The magnitude of that risk would depend on many factors, including the geopolitical intentions of Soviet leaders. Speculation about the likely course of action of the U.S.S.R. in the face of reduced or nonexistent nuclear defenses in the West is the responsibility of experts in diplomacy and military strategy and in diplomatic and military history. The answers to such questions are not by themselves moral judgments. They do bear upon the moral argument for unilateral disarmament, just as they are themselves subject to moral judgment.

The risk of unilateral nuclear disarmament could be very great indeed—surrender to totalitarian oppression. Alain Enthoven, Deputy Assistant Secretary of Defense in the Kennedy administration, defended the morality of nuclear deterrence in 1963 by arguing from the consequences of unilateral nuclear disarmament back to the validity of armed preparedness:

> Some people believe that we should reject the use of nuclear weapons altogether. Before accepting such a judgment, one should consider carefully the full implications of such a decision. We do have world-wide responsibilities. Many millions of people depend for their lives and freedom on our military strength. ("Reason, Morality and Defense Policy," *America*, 13 April 1963, p. 496)

Enthoven stressed the U.S. commitment to defend many people against the great evil of "totalitarianism and compulsory atheistic materialism enforced by the machinery of the modern police state" (ibid.). Since nuclear weapons are what they are, the best we can achieve, according to Enthoven, is "reconciliation of the traditional doctrine [of defense] with the facts of life in the nuclear age." This reconciliation is possible and morally defensible with a "U.S. defense policy, which emphasizes deterrence, control and the use of the appropriately limited amount of force" (p. 497).

Debate over unilateral nuclear disarmament may turn on questions of fact rather than on questions of moral principle. If the risk to the West is appraised as unacceptably high, then unilateral nuclear disarmament might be a morally attractive but morally unacceptable policy. If unilateral nuclear disarmament would, on the other hand, begin to reduce military risks and threats in the world, such a policy would be morally imperative.

But if nuclear weapons are essentially evil and must be abolished regardless of consequences, then the argument from the consequences of disarmament can be rejected outright. This position would properly be labeled nuclear pacifism, for it resembles strict pacifism, without compromise.

Discussion Questions

1. If the United States were to accept nuclear pacifism, how would that affect its policies on conventional armaments?
2. If the United States were to adopt a "no first use" policy for nuclear weapons, would potential enemies derive any advantage? Would the United States or its allies derive any advantage?
3. Would the use of tactical nuclear weapons be likely to escalate to the use of strategic nuclear weapons? What does your answer imply about the moral status of tactical nuclear

weapons?

4. What responsibilities has the United States to defend western Europe? Do these responsibilities require the deployment of nuclear weapons?
5. Roman Catholic Archbishop Raymond Hunthausen called unilateral nuclear disarmament "a moral imperative for followers of Christ." Do you agree, or disagree?
6. Why do some advocates of nuclear disarmament withhold a portion of their federal income taxes? Is this action likely to have an effect on United States' nuclear policy?

10

THE JUST-WAR THEORY

Will It Work in the Nuclear Age?

When the Empire of Japan attacked Pearl Harbor on December 7, 1941, the United States responded swiftly with a declaration of war. Little time was spent debating whether a war against Japan and its ally, Nazi Germany, would be morally justified. America judged that moral principle allowed and the defense of America demanded that the war be fought. This judgment— that the war would be a just war—was shared by an overwhelming majority of Americans; only a handful of strict pacifists disagreed.

Had a person paused to construct a moral justification of U.S. entry into World War II, the outline of the argument would have been readily available. That outline is the set of moral principles known as the just-war theory, which was developed over many centuries by Christian philosophers and theologians—Augustine of Hippo and Thomas Aquinas, in particular—who wished to apply the principles of justice to war. Justice, according to this kind of thinking, needs to be brought to bear both in the decision of whether or not a nation will go to war and in the decisions made during the conduct of the war. The former application of justice to war, called *jus ad bellum* in Latin, has seven requirements: just cause, lawful authority, right intention, just means, reasonable hope of success, last resort, and proportionality. All seven conditions must be met for a war to be considered just according to the theory.

These principles might have been applied to the decision by the United States to fight World War II.

1. *Just cause*. A nation's cause is most just when it is defending itself against armed aggression, equally just when

it defends innocent allies who are the victims of such aggression. The theory simply recognizes one of the primary functions of the government of a sovereign nation—protection of national security. At Pearl Harbor the Japanese attacked U.S. citizens and military forces directly; since 1939, allies of the United States, including Britain and France, had been under attack by Germany. An armed defense against these aggressions readily meets the just-cause condition of the just-war theory.

2. *Lawful authority.* In 1941 the United States had been organized as a sovereign nation for 165 years, ever since the British colonies in North America declared their independence from the mother country. Ever since 1789, the nation had been governed by a single Constitution, which grants to the Congress the authority to declare war and to the President the authority to be Commander-in-Chief of the armed forces. It seems clear that the U.S. government was legitimate and that it had authority to order an armed defense of the country.

3. *Right intention.* Intentions of nations vary with their leaders, with the mood of their people, with the circumstances of the moment. Certainly the primary intention of the U.S. declaration of war in 1941 was to bring the German and Japanese aggressions to a halt and restore peace among the nations. This intention meets the requirement of right intention under the just-war theory.

4. *Just means.* The first aim of a defensive war is to immobilize or destroy the armed might of the enemy. In the twentieth century that means sinking ships, shooting down airplanes, invading military installations, and killing enemy soldiers in the process. It may also include invasion of enemy territory in order to induce the war leaders to cease their war making. All these means involve the violent killing or injuring of human beings. Thus the justification of defensive war leads to a justification of taking lives or at least violently attacking other people in the process. Definite restrictions apply: Not all citizens of the enemy country are responsible for the aggression

or are involved in it; these innocent persons must not be attacked or killed. Nor are certain methods of treating enemy
soldiers—such as torture—morally acceptable. When World
War II began for the United States, the conventional albeit
brutal capabilities of modern warfare were available to both
sides in the conflict, and the use of these means by the United
States seemed then (and now) to be morally acceptable. As
that conflict wore on, however, other means became available
and were used—including counter-city bombing with TNT
and incendiary bombs, and finally with atomic bombs. Whether
the new means were immoral under the circumstances and
whether, if so, the U.S. role in the war then lost its moral
justification are debated to this day.

5. *Reasonable hope of success.* The United States in 1941
was an industrialized nation, capable of producing large quan-
tities of effective weapons and other wartime equipment. Its
citizens appeared quite prepared to go to war. Neither the
Japanese nor the Germans seemed to possess any invulnerable
offensive or defensive force. So Americans could reasonably
expect to win the war. At no time during World War II did
the American hope of victory turn to despair.

6. *Last resort.* Could the United States and the Allies have
settled the differences between themselves and the Axis powers
by any means short of war? Britain had tried peaceful negotiations with Germany in the middle 1930s, a process that
became known contemptuously as "appeasement." In the Pacific, the United States and Japan had carried on a policy of
action and reaction that led nowhere; meanwhile in Japan a
war party successfully pressed for an armed attack on the
United States. After the 1939 Nazi invasions in Europe and
the Japanese attack on Pearl Harbor two years later, no other
opportunities for peaceful settlements existed. For the United
States to declare war in 1941 could properly be called a last
resort.

7. *Proportionality.* The aim of this requirement of just-war
theory has been described by James Turner Johnson of Rutgers
University: "to ensure that the overall damage to human values

that ensues from resort to force will be at least balanced by the degree to which human values are preserved or protected" ("What Guidance Can Just War Tradition Provide for Contemporary Moral Thought About War?" *New Catholic World*, March-April 1982, p. 84). Proportionality asks that two elements be weighed in the balance—damage done in the war and protection of human values achieved by the war. Unfortunately, there is no single gauge to measure these two elements; yet the comparison is forced upon a nation that is deciding whether engaging in a particular war will be moral. In World War II, the potential damage to human values at the hand of the Japanese and the Germans was truly gigantic; but what destruction would be inflicted by the United States to protect against that damage was not clearly known at the outset of the war. Potentially the destruction could be limited, but that limit depended on the ferocity with which Japan and Germany would prolong the war, especially if it went against them. As events worked out, the destruction visited upon Germany by means of strategic bombing and upon Japan by incendiary and finally atomic bombing was extensive. After the war most Americans believed that protection from the tyranny of Japan and Germany had been worth the price. Proportionality also requires that the particular means of warfare—the weapons— be justifiable by a balance between their destructiveness and their good effects. To many people today, counter-city obliteration bombing, including the bombing of Hiroshima and Nagasaki, seems to have violated this principle, but during World War II many believed the bombing was permissible.

Nuclear weapons created a new set of moral questions and, in the opinion of some moral philosophers and theologians, a challenge to the just-war theory itself. It may be argued that once the use of strategic nuclear weapons is contemplated, fulfillment of all of the seven just war conditions becomes impossible. But *tactical* nuclear weapons must also be considered; then the just-war criteria, though very difficult, are perhaps not impossible to fulfill.

In 1981 the Roman Catholic bishop of Cleveland, Anthony
M. Pilla, applied traditional just-war criteria to the possibility
of nuclear war. Tracing the theory to Augustine of Hippo, he
summarized the just-war theory in six statements:

1. The decision for war must be made by a legitimate
   authority.
2. The war must be fought for a just cause.
3. War must be taken only as a last resort.
4. There must be a reasonable chance of "success."
5. The good to be achieved by the war must outweigh
   the evil that will result from it. (Proportionality)
6. The war must be waged with just means (in accor-
   dance with natural and international law). (Heyer, *Key
   Statements,* p. 145)

Bishop Pilla then brought these principles to bear on the
possibility of nuclear war:

Nuclear weapons made possible the total destruction of
entire innocent civilian populations in a very short amount
of time. Not only was such annihilation against rules 5
and 6 of the just war doctrine, it far overstepped rule 4
by giving the aggressor overwhelming odds for success.
Also, the simplicity and power of one atomic warhead
made rule 1, assent of a legitimate authority, and rule 2,
need for a just cause for aggression, easily bypassable
by anyone in control of a bomb. Finally, the presence of
nuclear technology led to the "first strike" philosophy
and the arms race, thus negating rule 3. (Pp. 145-46)

Pilla concluded from his analysis: "So nuclear weapons
clearly break all St. Augustine's standards for justice" (ibid.).
Evidently Bishop Pilla considered only strategic nuclear
weapons—and thus only counter-city nuclear warfare—in his
analysis; for tactical weapons and counter-force warfare would
not totally destroy "entire innocent civilian populations."
Moreover, what Pilla evidently understands by the requirements for lawful authorization of war and for a just cause for

going to war seems not to fit the situation of a nation defending itself against aggression. Such hypothetical disagreements with Pilla's analysis illustrate that just-war theory is debatable when applied to nuclear war and nuclear weapons.

Yet other religious leaders have simply concluded that just-war criteria are inapplicable to nuclear warfare. Roman Catholic Archbishop John R. Quinn of San Francisco said in 1981: "If we apply each of [the] traditional principles of [just-war theory] to the current international arms race, we must conclude that a 'just' nuclear war is a contradiction in terms" (p. 161). Quinn singled out the criteria of proportionality and just means to underscore his point. He also appeared to have in mind strategic nuclear weapons and counter-city warfare. Yet the phrase "a contradiction in terms" seems to suggest that when nuclear weapons are considered, none of the just-war principles can possibly apply. This is another debatable point, since tactical weapons and counter-force warfare need to be included in the discussion.

The just-war theory remains a useful set of moral principles, however; it provides guidance today, even though the theory leads persons to differing conclusions. Some conclude that all forms of nuclear war would violate justice; but other thinkers conclude that some forms of nuclear war might be morally justifiable. This latter conclusion appears to have persuaded certain leaders in the Roman Catholic Church to doubt and criticize the just-war theory itself. Bishop Walter Sullivan of Richmond, Virginia, characterized the theory as "an excuse to go to war, mental gymnastics, casuistry of the worst sort" (*National Catholic Reporter*, 11 Dec. 1981). Although Bishop Sullivan may have had nuclear war in mind, his dismissal of the theory as such would seem to ban all conventional war also. Bishop Carroll Dozier of Memphis, Tennessee, in a speech to the 1982 national meeting of Pax Christi U.S.A., asserted that "the just-war theory should be put into a drawer along with the flat-earth theory."

The National Conference of Catholic Bishops reasserted the centrality of the just-war theory in Roman Catholic teaching in their pastoral letter, *The Challenge of Peace*. But they also acknowledged the "support for a pacifist option for individuals in the teaching of Vatican II and the reaffirmation that the popes have given to non-violent witness since the time of the council" (*Challenge*, p. 12). And although pacifism and the just-war ethic are incompatible in principle, the bishops believe that "the two perspectives support and complement one another, each preserving the other from distortion" (ibid.).

Of the just-war theory itself, the pastoral says:

> Just war teaching has evolved . . . as an effort to prevent war; only if war cannot be rationally avoided does the teaching then seek to restrict and reduce its horrors. It does this by establishing a set of rigorous conditions which must be met if the decision to go to war is to be morally permissible. Such a decision, especially today, requires extraordinarily strong reasons for overriding the presumption *in favor of peace* and *against* war. . . . It is presumed that all sane people prefer peace, never *want* to initiate war and accept even the most justifiable defensive war only as a sad necessity. Only the most powerful reasons may be permitted to override such objection. (*Challenge*, p. 10)

According to the bishops, the just-war theory aims to prevent war by placing the burden of proof on any person or nation claiming that a particular war is morally acceptable. Individuals contemplating participating in a war would thus be required to reach a moral judgment beforehand rather than assuming that whatever one's country does is acceptable.

The bishops say that both pacifism and just-war principles seek to prevent war, and thus both positions morally condemn nuclear war: "As a people, we must refuse to legitimate the idea of nuclear war" (p. 13). This conclusion appears to derive, in part, from the argument that just-war principles make any form of nuclear war morally wrong under all circumstances.

The bishops reach two other conclusions with clarity and confidence:

Under no circumstances may nuclear weapons or other instruments of mass slaughter be used for the purpose of destroying population centers or other predominantly civilian targets. (Pp. 14-15)

We do not perceive any situation in which the deliberate initiation of nuclear warfare on however restricted a scale can be morally justified. (P. 15)

Both of these practical moral conclusions can be inferred from the just-war principles. A thread of just-war thinking runs through the pastoral letter, beginning with approval of the just-war theory and continuing through the moral outlawing of counter-city warfare and first nuclear strikes.

That the bishops and others run into difficulties with the idea of limited defensive nuclear war and with the more subtle issues of nuclear deterrence does not prove that the just-war theory is flawed nor that it must be abandoned, as Bishops Sullivan and Dozier would have it. It should be recognized that the *jus ad bellum* aspect of the just-war theory discussed here is limited to deciding whether a specific war would be morally acceptable. It does not address other moral problems associated with war—the risk of war caused by the buildup of armaments, for example, or the need for defensive capability in the face of aggressive neighboring nations, or the legitimacy of revolutionary violence. In the nuclear age, many of these moral problems, along with the decision of a nation to declare war against another nation, are nonetheless intense and badly in need of analysis.

Nuclear deterrence raises a very difficult moral problem that neither the just-war theory nor pacifism can solve. The U.S. deterrence force is intended to prevent nuclear aggression; thus it fulfills the goal of the just-war theory as understood by the

American Roman Catholic bishops: to prevent war. But a nuclear deterrent runs grave risks: accidental discharge of missiles, for example, or provocation of potential enemies similarly armed, or overreaction when some defense of the United States less destructive than nuclear retaliation would satisfy. Whether these risks are acceptable morally is a vital question today, but the just-war theory cannot provide the answers. The most to be expected is that its application to such problems as deterrence will invite distinctions worthy of study and thought.

The just-war theory in effect asserts that justice is the chief test to be applied to the limits of war. Pacifism holds that Christian love is the standard. Adherents of the just-war theory, therefore, might be more ready than pacifists to weigh the risks posed by a nuclear deterrent, since the principles of justice are commonly used to adjudicate conflicting claims of individuals and groups.

Some have decided that the just-war theory must somehow be transcended in the nuclear age, that as a theory it may be valid but that nuclear weapons make it less useful or perhaps not useful at all. Major General Kermit D. Johnson, who was chief of chaplains of the U.S. Army, has described the development of his position in the matter. He had been a commissioner to the General Assembly of the United Presbyterian Church in 1980 when it adopted a statement entitled "The Call to Peacemaking." This statement did not mention justice or the just-war theory. General Johnson later wrote: "I saw 'The Call to Peacemaking' document as pacifistic and deficient in its failure to affirm the 'just war'" ("The Nuclear Reality: Beyond Niebuhr and the Just War," *The Christian Century,* 13 Oct. 1982, p. 1014). But two years later Johnson announced that his "view of nuclear war and nuclear weapons" had changed (ibid.). He explained his new understanding of the place of just-war theory:

> The nuclear reality . . . takes us beyond the "just war" as a justification or rationalization for the use of nuclear weapons. Nuclear war is indicted, not vindicated, by the

limiting categories of just-war criteria such as due proportion, just means, just intentions and reasonable possibility of success. (Ibid., p. 1015)

General Johnson discusses the question of applying just-war principles to limited counter-force nuclear war. This kind of war may be morally permissible according to the just-war theory. But potential use of nuclear weapons as counter-force weapons, Johnson says, still leaves unsolved the question of escalation: "How can we know that *any* use of nuclear weapons will not result in catastrophic escalation?" (ibid.) He then seems to go beyond the just-war theory: "The technical discussions as to when or whether nuclear weapons can be used without violating just war criteria are irrelevant unless the question of escalation can be answered with certainty" (ibid.).

In what sense has General Johnson's thinking gone beyond the just-war theory? Insofar as "nuclear warfare is indicted, not vindicated," the theory continues to offer the moral guidance always intended. But if discussions of the justice of limited use of counter-force nuclear weapons are actually irrelevant without first settling the question of the risks of escalation, is the theory bypassed? Possibly not, for the just-war theory was never meant to be a way to estimate risks. If nuclear weapons pose special problems such as the risk of escalation that the just-war theory is not meant to solve, we have not gone beyond that theory. Instead, the existence of nuclear armaments has generated moral issues even more difficult than those included in just-war theory. The theory would still apply insofar as it stipulates—according to General Johnson—that if escalation is likely when counter-force nuclear weapons are used, then even limited use of tactical nuclear weapons would be immoral.

If in any sense the concept of just war is abandoned, it will still remain very important not to abandon the concept of justice in the process. For relations between nations have moral qualities that always need to be measured against justice.

Discussion Questions

1. The just-war theory specifies seven conditions that must be fulfilled before a nation can legitimately go to war. Has any war the U.S. has engaged in met all these conditions?
2. If a government decides to go to war, what are the dangers if every citizen presumes that the war is just? What are the dangers if every citizen makes up his or her own mind on the justice of the war?
3. Can any form of nuclear war be justified by the criteria of the just-war theory?
4. Can just-war principles be applied to the question of whether a nuclear deterrent is a morally acceptable policy for the United States? If so, how?
5. Is the just-war theory still valid in the era of nuclear weapons and intercontinental ballistic missiles?
6. If the just-war theory is abandoned, what criteria are available to guide moral judgments about wars?

11

NATIONAL DEFENSE

A Single Moral Imperative?

It has been commonly accepted that a sovereign nation has the right and duty to defend itself against aggression and oppression by other nations. That right and duty, when perceived to be a nation's single moral imperative, is the source of strong support for justifying war, including nuclear war, the arms race, and nuclear weapons themselves.

"Eternal vigilance is the price of liberty." This dictum of Thomas Jefferson expresses that the world of sovereign nations is a world of risks, a world in which nations must always anticipate the possibility of aggression from others. Thomas Hobbes, writing in the seventeenth century, described the relationship of nations as a "state of war," in which no laws exist to which the member nations can subscribe. In such a situation, according to Hobbes, self-interest will be the primary motivation; and self-interest certainly accurately describes the history of nation-states. History also shows that a primary objective of a self-interested person or nation is self-defense.

In the modern world, risks always inherent in the system of sovereign nations increased as the technology of new weapons developed. Two developments in the post-World War II era created great new risks: the nuclear bomb and the intercontinental missile. Nations can now threaten to annihilate entire cities within a few minutes after deciding to attack. The mere threat of nuclear aggression can intimidate other nations even without direct attack.

When nuclear weapons are in the hands of an aggressor, other countries face a most difficult question: How can adequate defenses be erected against the potential of nuclear attack? This question has faced the United States ever since the Soviet Union exploded its first nuclear bomb in 1949. In the aftermath of World War II, the U.S.S.R. committed terrible aggression upon its neighbors. It continues to hold officially to an ideology that seems to threaten still other aggressions in the future.

For more than thirty years, the United States government has responded to potential nuclear aggression without much deviation of policy. The paramount consideration for government leaders working in this area has always been to guarantee national security, to be able to respond to aggression with sufficient military might to discourage or defeat any aggressor. The moral basis claimed for such policies is the nation's duty to defend its citizens and territory, with military force if necessary. The strength of this national will is exemplified by a sentence from the inaugural address of President John F. Kennedy in 1961: "Let every nation know, whether it wishes us well or ill, that we shall pay any price, bear any burden, meet any hardship, support any friend, oppose any foe, in order to assure the survival and the success of liberty."

Against a potential aggressor armed with nuclear weapons, there seems—from that point of view—to be no choice other than to possess nuclear weapons and missiles to discourage or defeat aggression. Any sane aggressor would hesitate to destroy a city of another nation if it knew that retaliation would be quick and certain. Thus a nation such as the United States, equipped with a nuclear-armed missile force, can be understood to possess a huge deterrent to any aggression with nuclear weapons by a nation such as the Soviet Union. If only nuclear weapons will deter nuclear aggression, then building and deploying American nuclear missiles becomes, in the view of many, a sure practical consequence of the moral mandate to defend the nation.

Americans with this understanding of the moral imperative of national defense often point to the fact that in the past four decades no nuclear weapon has been used in warfare, even though many wars—some involving the United States—have been waged around the world. Such persons argue that if nuclear deterrence is not only morally required but practically successful, it is clearly a desirable policy for the present and near future. Proponents of the moral primacy of national defense admit the risks involved, but they find them acceptable. John P. Lehman, Jr., Secretary of the Navy in the Reagan administration, has written:

> Except for the pacifists, most philosophers—and most nations—have reasoned that self-defense was a moral risk worth taking compared to the immorality of submission to aggression, with its certain loss of innocent lives and liberty. Nearly 40 years of experience with nuclear deterrence have not changed this conviction. (*Wall Street Journal*, 16 Nov. 1982)

In the debate over the morality of nuclear arms, extreme positions have a common element—the belief that martyrdom is the ultimate test of morality. Christian martyrs honored in every century have testified to a deep belief that there are ideas worth dying for. Both those who hold that death is preferable to immoral use of nuclear weapons and those who hold that death by nuclear war is preferable to immoral oppression invoke Christian ideals to justify their position.

Thomas J. Reese, S.J., an associate editor of *America*, has written of his pacifist view of martyrdom:

> Bluntly put, I believe that surrender to Communist domination is preferable to the destruction of the world, even if this resulted in a persecution of Christians to match the Nazi persecution of the Jews. . . . Eventually Christianity would triumph just as it did over the barbarians. ("The Third Draft of the Peace Proposal," *America*, 23 April 1983, p. 321)

And from the perspective of the prime importance of national defense, Alan L. Keyes, a staff member of the State Department's Foreign Policy Planning Council, has written:

The voluntary fate embraced by the early Christian martyrs suggests that there must be a dimension to moral action, especially in the Christian tradition, that goes beyond calculations of physical danger and fear in order to take account of spiritual goods that are no less real for being intangible. . . . If the physical horrors of nuclear war were endured or risked for the sake of such values, would this intention have no relevance to the character of the choice that permitted such a war to occur? ("The Morality of Deterrence," *Catholicism in Crisis*, April 1983, p. 34)

The conviction that morality demands an effective national defense, including nuclear defense against potential nuclear attack, often accompanies a harsh view of the Soviet Union. This view sees the Soviet government as ruthless, expansionist, threatening to its neighbors and to much of the world, and cynical about Western efforts to reduce armaments. The Soviets came to possess nuclear weapons later than the United States but developed and deployed them rapidly in the 1960s and 1970s. Harold Brown, Secretary of Defense in the Carter administration, once gave his capsule view of Soviet arms policy: "When we build, they build. When we stop building, they build."

Through the 1970s the American nuclear arsenal was decreased in some of its components and grew little or not at all in others. By the time the SALT II treaty was negotiated in the late 1970s, the U.S.S.R. had reached approximate nuclear parity with the United States. Regarding this situation as dangerous to world peace, the Reagan administration proposed a new buildup of American arms, both conventional and nuclear. The rationale for this policy was derived from the same moral conviction that guided previous administrations in their deterrence policy: the conviction that the demands of world peace and national security imply a moral imperative to use American armed might to discourage the Soviet Union from any temptation to use its weapons of war. To permit the Soviets superiority in nuclear weapons would arouse their aggressive tendencies, according to this idea. Any U.S. policy leading to such a result would therefore be immoral.

The Reagan administration took an opportunity to declare its moral viewpoint when the National Conference of Catholic Bishops met in November 1982 to discuss its draft pastoral letter on war and peace. William P. Clark, the president's national security adviser, sent a letter to the bishops on behalf of President Ronald Reagan, Secretary of State George Schultz, Secretary of Defense Caspar Weinberger, and others, in which the administration associated itself with some of the bishops' goals: "We share an enormous sense of responsibility for the protection of our people and our values." Clark referred to the pastoral's assertions that, to be moral, defense policy must seek to prevent war and to take arms control and disarmament more likely:

> We believe that our weapons systems (which are not designed to be "first-strike" systems), our deterrence posture (which is defensive), and our arms control initiatives (which call for deep and verifiable reductions) do conform to these objectives. (*New York Times*, 17 Nov. 1982)

Against a Soviet threat, proponents of a strong national defense argue, a deterrent must be credible in blunt military terms; the very existence of this deterrent must be such as to dissuade aggressive leaders in the Soviet Union from attempting any actions that would endanger the United States or its allies. Therefore, they say, deterrence would be undermined if its intentions were to be condemned as immoral. Much recent writing asserts that intending to use nuclear weapons is as morally wrong as actually using them. Michael Novak, a Catholic philosopher, has responded to this argument as a proponent of a stronger national defense. The Roman Catholic bishops,

Novak has written,

> argue that a deterrent is morally permissible, but only if
> one never *intends* or *threatens* to use it. Nuclear weapons
> they say may *never* be *used* (in any of the most likely
> circumstances of use). Possibly this is a semantic mis-
> take. Perhaps the bishops mean by *intention* and *threat*
> words or thoughts only. In an architectonic system of
> readiness, however, there is another sort of *intention* and
> *threat* far more credible than mind-reading. Readiness
> itself is the only real intention, the only real threat, which
> a distant adversary can take seriously. Adversaries ignore
> words. ("Making Deterrence Work," *Catholicism in Cri-
> sis*, Nov. 1982, p. 4)

According to this line of argument, the moral acceptability
of defense policies and weapons systems is based on the primary moral imperative to defend the nation effectively against
any potential aggressor. William Clark defended the morality
of the Reagan administration's nuclear policy:

> It is important for the Bishops Conference to know our
> decisions on nuclear armaments, and our defense posture
> are guided by moral considerations as compelling as any
> which have faced mankind. The strategy of deterrence
> on which our policies are based is not an end in itself
> but a means to prevent war and preserve the values we
> cherish: respect for the sanctity of human life and the
> rule of law through representative institutions. (*New York
> Times*, 17 Nov. 1982)

From this perspective, the arms race, far from being a "false
and dangerous program" as it was described by Pope Paul VI
(*Key Statements*, p. 32), must be won by the United States if
aggression is to be deterred.

Denunciations of the arms race such as Paul VI's often leave
room for balance, however; in 1978 Paul VI told the United
Nations General Assembly that "one can and must endeavor
to reduce mutually the arsenals of war, in a way that does not

destroy the existing balances . . ." (ibid., p. 36). Pope John Paul II has continued to express this view; in 1982 he said to the United Nations General Assembly:

> In current conditions, deterrence based on balance, certainly not as an end in itself but as a step toward progressive disarmament, may still be judged morally acceptable. (*Origins*, 21 Oct. 1982, p. 293)

Balancing arsenals of war is unacceptable to many who hold to the moral imperative of national defense as a primary moral principle. Because they believe that the Soviet Union is the most threatening nation in the world, they would insist that the United States strive to be more powerful than the Soviet Union. Yet balance of arms is what now obtains between the superpowers, roughly speaking; and some hold that the balance may be as successful in maintaining an overall peace as was the relative dominance of the United States in decades past.

Proponents of nuclear superiority for the United States must also face the objection that striving for superiority over the U.S.S.R. will likely result in a more and more dangerous world. To accumulate weaponry capable of destroying the Soviet Union many times over may, moreover, add little or nothing to the true defense of the United States. It may also waste resources that are badly needed for other priorities. Advocates of a stronger national military strength as a moral imperative often respond to these objections by casting blame on the Soviet Union and by claiming to know of no better alternative than the arms race.

The moral perspective of the Reagan administration finds much to criticize in the movement for a freeze on the development and deployment of nuclear weapons. If the freeze recommended were to be unilateral, it would be unreservedly condemned from this perspective. Advocates of a stronger national defense also tend to oppose a bilateral freeze. Senator Henry M. Jackson, Democrat of Washington, spoke against a freeze resolution in the U.S. Senate on May 12, 1982:

> For many of us a freeze on nuclear forces at their present
> levels of threat and terror perpetuates the very problem
> we are trying to solve. Indeed, we would severely lessen
> the chances for real arms reductions if ever we adopted
> policies ratifying or acquiescing in or legitimizing the
> nuclear armaments status quo. (*Congressional Digest,*
> Aug.-Sept. 1982, p. 203)

What could be wrong with stopping nuclear armaments at
the status quo? Senator Jake Garn, Republican of Utah, speaking on May 13, 1982, in effect responded to this question:

> A nuclear freeze on the testing, production, and further
> deployment of nuclear warheads, missiles, and other de-
> livery systems sounds simple enough, but where does it
> get us? Quite frankly, it gets us nowhere. It does not
> resolve the vulnerability problem of our ICBM force, it
> does not provide us with an effective replacement for our
> aging B-52 force, it does not allow us to deploy survivable
> air-launched cruise missiles, it does not place any re-
> straints on Soviet air defense systems, and it does not
> allow us to restore the nuclear balance in Europe. (Ibid.,
> p. 215)

Senator Garn summarized his opposition to the freeze resolution: "In short, it does nothing to enhance the security of
this country or its allies" (ibid.). In other words, opponents
of the freeze judge the proposal on whether it helps or harms
the national defense of the United States.

Freeze opponents, however, do not see their disagreement
with the backers of the freeze as a difference of goals. In his
remarks to his Senate colleagues, Jackson said, "I do not see
how there can be any disagreement about the goal of our arms
negotiations with the Soviets" (ibid., p. 203). Jackson is no
doubt correct in believing that all parties to the debate wish
to reduce the levels of nuclear weapons and ultimately to abolish them altogether. But the differences may not be, as he says,

simply "the question of means and not . . . ends" (ibid.). Freeze proponents tend to rely on moral principles other than the single principle of national security.

Those who emphasize the moral duty of national defense accept, as Thomas Hobbes did three centuries ago, the division of the world into nation-states, each sovereign in its own sphere and responsible to its citizens for their safety. The world in fact is organized that way and can be expected to remain so in the near future. But must the arrangement of nation-states be permanent?

Jonathan Schell, in *The Fate of the Earth*, argues that the existence of sovereign nations and, in particular, the value placed on their sovereignty constitute a problem to be solved, not an unalterable fact. The world pays an enormous price, Schell writes, for "its insistence on continuing to divide itself up into sovereign nations"; that price, he believes, is "the peril of extinction" (*Fate*, p. 210). Nor is paying such an awful price inevitable, according to Schell. Rather, governments of the nation-states make the choice to prefer national sovereignty: "The nuclear powers put a higher value on national sovereignty than they do on human survival" (ibid.).

Thus, for Schell, the problem of nuclear weapons rests on the deeper and more stubborn problem of national sovereignty. National sovereignty, he writes, "lies at the very core of the political issues that the peril of extinction forces upon us" (p. 218). But Schell has no solution. He believes "we can choose to live in some other system," yet he accepts that that choice cannot be made without a "full-scale reexamination of the foundations of political thought" (p. 219).

Schell's prescription is readily criticized for its unrealistic expectations; for the entire world to reexamine its political foundations is no doubt virtually impossible. Yet there exists an organization, the United Nations, that provides a forum in which the nations of the world can speak with one another and attempt to come to mutually satisfactory agreements. Schell views the U.N. as only "the empty husk of . . . irresolute good intentions" to find a new approach to international disputes (p. 194). However, for many other moral thinkers concerned with the problems posed by nuclear weapons, the U.N. offers hope that perhaps the world's arrangement of sovereign nations can be made to work in the interests of peace rather than war.

The American Roman Catholic bishops, in *The Challenge of Peace*, put themselves squarely behind the efforts of the United Nations:

> Papal teaching of the last four decades has not only supported international institutions in principle, it has supported the United Nations specifically. . . . in light of the continuing endorsement found in papal teaching, we urge that the United States adopt a supportive leadership role with respect to the United Nations. (P. 25)

Despite this endorsement, the bishops are not satisfied with the U.N.'s effectiveness to guarantee world peace. There is still something missing in the arrangement of sovereign states: "An important element missing from world order today is a properly constituted political authority with the capacity to shape our material interdependence in the direction of moral interdependence" (p. 23). Whether the bishops are suggesting a world government or only a strengthened United Nations is not clear. What is clear is their dissatisfaction with the current arrangement of nation-states, a dissatisfaction not shared by proponents of national defense as the primary moral imperative.

The national-security perspective offers a view of the world's condition quite at odds with that of pacifists, nuclear pacifists, and proponents of a nuclear freeze. The national-security side of the debate looks at the world and finds it at peace—that is, without all-out war, nuclear war, or any war between the superpowers. Their opponents in the debate look at the same world and find dangers of nuclear war, escalation of armaments that seems to make war more likely and to make actual wars liable to occur at any time. Thus nuclear weapons can be seen from two opposite perspectives: One sees them bringing potential devastation and perhaps inevitable nuclear war; the other sees the weapons as dangerous but, by means of U.S. policies, as contributing to the current peace.

Erik Von Kuehnelt-Leddihn, an Austrian Roman Catholic who often writes on American affairs, has summarized the view of those who argue that the primary moral principle is national security:

> . . . World War III has not erupted. It has not erupted because both camps have been restrained by their knowledge of the potential magnitude of atomic destruction. This is called the balance of terror, and it has given us our precarious modus vivendi. If morality is to be measured by instrumental criteria, it is fair to say, as Winston Churchill did in 1949, that the atom bomb brought the world a measure of peace. ("Bishops on the Brink," *National Review*, 26 Nov. 1982, p. 1472)

The assertion that the atom bomb has brought peace to the world exhibits both ends of the spectrum of moral perspectives on nuclear armaments. Pacifists seek peace directly and strive to eliminate armaments; believers in military strength seek American superiority in nuclear weapons on the grounds that it will maintain peace. Although peace is the ultimate goal of all—those at opposite ends of the spectrum and those between—wide differences in applying moral principles and plans of action continue to separate concerned persons everywhere. Whether these differences can be reduced through exchanges of ideas is a question that challenges thinking people throughout the world. But as human thinking produced nuclear weapons, so must human thinking rise to the challenge of conquering the dangers they now pose. As George F. Kennan wrote in "A Christian's View of the Arms Race" in *Theology Today* in July 1982, "The public discussion of the problems presented by nuclear weaponry which is now taking place in this country is going to go down in history, I suspect . . , as the most significant that any democratic society has ever engaged in"

(p. 162). To the significance of the debate Leon Wieseltier added an imperative in *The New Republic* in January 1983: "If there is anything as foolish as not thinking about nuclear weapons, it is not thinking about them enough" (p. 7).

Discussion Questions

1. If a nation's single moral imperative is national defense, can anything and everything be deemed morally acceptable when done in the name of national defense? What are the limits to the means of defense?
2. If it were possible for the United States to "win" the nuclear arms race, what might the result be? Would it be desirable?
3. Is the sovereignty of nation-states a source of the nuclear-weapons problem? Is there a need for some limits on national sovereignty in order to deal with this problem? Or are sovereign nations as we know them better able to deal with the problem of nuclear weapons?
4. What specific steps could the United Nations take to reduce the dangers of nuclear war?
5. To what extent is the danger of nuclear war the responsibility of the Soviet Union? How should the United States respond to the threats of the Soviets?
6. Will the cause of world peace be best served by a nuclear balance of terror between the United States and the Soviet Union? By bilateral reductions in armaments? By nuclear superiority of the United States?

NOTES

Introduction

1. Robert Heyer, ed., *Nuclear Disarmament: Key Statements of Popes, Bishops, Councils and Churches* (New York: Paulist Press, 1982), p. 255. Hereafter referred to as *Key Statements*.
2. "The Challenge of Peace: God's Promise and Our Response," *Origins*, 19 May 1983, p. 26. Hereafter referred to as *Challenge*.
3. *Frontiers in American Democracy* (Cleveland: World Publishing Co., 1960), pp. 38, 59.

Chapter 1   The Nuclear Era Opens: The 1940s and 1950s

1. Nuel Pharr Davis, *Lawrence and Oppenheimer* (New York: Simon and Schuster, 1968), p. 250.
2. *Atomic Quest: A Personal Narrative* (New York: Oxford University Press, 1956), p. 240. Hereafter referred to as *Atomic Quest*.
3. Herbert Feis, *Japan Subdued: The Atomic Bomb and the End of the War in the Pacific* (Princeton, N.J.: Princeton University Press, 1961), p. 94.
4. *Year of Decisions* (Garden City, N.Y.: Doubleday and Co., 1955), pp. 419-20.
5. Herbert F. York, *The Advisors: Oppenheimer, Teller and the Superbomb* (San Francisco: W. H. Freeman and Co., 1976), p. 155. Hereafter referred to as *Advisors*.
6. Harry S Truman, *Years of Trial and Hope* (Garden City, N.Y.: Doubleday and Co., 1956), p. 309.
7. *Hiroshima* (New York: Knopf, 1981), pp. 117-18.

Chapter 2   Missiles and Negotiations: The 1960s and 1970s

1. Paul Ramsey, *The Limits of Nuclear War: Thinking About the Do-*

Able and the Un-Do-Able (New York: The Council on Religion and International Affairs, 1963), p. 7. Hereafter referred to as *Limits*.
2. *Pacem in Terris* (New York: Paulist Press, 1963), p. 39.
3. Michael Mandelbaum, *The Nuclear Question: The United States and Nuclear Weapons, 1946-1976* (Cambridge: Cambridge University Press, 1979), p. 176.
4. T. B. Millar, *The East-West Strategic Balance* (London: George Allen and Unwin, 1981), p. 50.

Chapter 3   Nuclear War: Counter-city and Counter-force

1. *The Fate of the Earth* (New York: Avon Books, 1982), pp. 56-57. Hereafter referred to as *Fate*.
2. Jim Wallis, ed., *Waging Peace: A Handbook for the Struggle to Abolish Nuclear Weapons* (San Francisco: Harper and Row, 1982), p. 81. Hereafter referred to as *Waging Peace*.
3. Austin Fagothey, S.J., *Right and Reason: Ethics in Theory and Practice* (St. Louis: The C. V. Mosby Co., 1959), pp. 153-54.

Chapter 5   Disarmament: How to Call Off the Arms Race

1. John Donaghy, ed., *To Proclaim Peace: Religious Statements on the Arms Race* (Nyack, N.Y.: Fellowship of Reconciliation, 1981), p. 20. Hereafter referred to as *Peace*.

Chapter 6   Possession of Nuclear Weapons: Tolerable, or Not?

1. NCCB, "God's Hope in a Time of Fear" (mimeo), p. 31. Hereafter referred to as *God's Hope*.

Chapter 8   Pacifism and Nonviolence: Ideal, or Mandate?

1. *Catholicism* (Minneapolis: Winston Press, 1980), p. 1035.

2. Thomas A. Shannon, ed., *War or Peace? The Search for New Answers* (Maryknoll, N.Y.: Orbis Books, 1980), p. 225. Hereafter referred to as *War or Peace*.

3. *Making the Abolition of War a Realistic Goal* (New York: Institute for World Order, 1980), p. 3. Hereafter referred to as *Abolition*.

FURTHER READING

Adams, Ruth, and Susan Cullen, eds. *The Final Epidemic: Physicians and Scientists on Nuclear War.* Chicago: University of Chicago Press, 1982.

Barash, David P., and Judith Eve Lipton. *Stop Nuclear War! A Handbook.* New York: Grove Press, 1982.

Contains extensive lists of organizations—with addresses—devoted to action against the nuclear arms race, including nuclear-freeze offices in most states.

Beres, Louis René. *Mimicking Sisyphus: America's Countervailing Nuclear Strategy.* Lexington, Mass.: Lexington Books, 1982.

Cesaretti, C. A., and Joseph T. Vitale, eds. *Rumors of War: A Moral and Theological Perspective on the Arms Race.* New York: Seabury Press, 1982.

Chivan, Eric, et al., eds. *Last Aid: The Medical Dimensions of Nuclear War.* San Francisco: W. H. Freeman and Co., 1982.

A collection of essays by physicians and others. Most were presented as papers at the First Congress of International Physicians for the Prevention of Nuclear War, held in Washington, D.C., in March 1981. Includes a list of delegates to the Congress.

The Church and the Bomb: Nuclear Weapons and the Christian Conscience. London: CIO Press, 1982.

Clark, Ronald W. *The Greatest Power on Earth: The International Race for Nuclear Supremacy.* New York: Harper and Row, 1982.

Clarke, Michael, and Marjorie Mowlam, eds. *Debate on Disarmament*. London: Routledge and Kegan Paul, 1982.

Drinan, Robert F., S.J. *Beyond the Nuclear Freeze*. New York: Seabury Press, 1983.

Ford, Daniel, Henry Kendall, and Steven Nadis. *Beyond the Freeze: The Road to Nuclear Sanity*. Boston: Beacon Press, 1982.

Freedman, Lawrence. *The Evolution of Nuclear Strategy*. New York: St. Martin's Press, 1981.

Geyer, Alan. *The Idea of Disarmament! Rethinking the Unthinkable*. Elgin, Ill.: Brethren Press, 1982.

Goodwin, Geoffrey, ed. *Ethics and Nuclear Deterrence*. New York: St. Martin's Press, 1982.

Ground Zero. *Nuclear War: What's in It for You?* New York: Pocket Books, 1982.
The "primary educational resource" of the Ground Zero Organization. Contains a glossary of nuclear-war terms.

Heyer, Robert, ed. *Nuclear Disarmament: Key Statements of Popes, Bishops, Councils and Churches*. New York: Paulist Press, 1982.

Johnson, James Turner. *Just War Tradition and the Restraint of War: A Moral and Historical Inquiry*. Princeton, N.J.: Princeton University Press, 1981.

Kennan, George F. *The Nuclear Delusion: Soviet-American Relations in the Atomic Age*. New York: Pantheon Books, 1982.

Essays by a former ambassador to the Soviet Union, currently Professor Emeritus at the Institute for Advanced Study, Princeton. The essays were written between 1950 and 1982.

Kennedy, Edward M., and Mark O. Hatfield. *Freeze! How You Can Help Prevent Nuclear War.* New York: Bantam Books, 1982.

The case for a nuclear freeze by two U.S. senators who were authors of a congressional nuclear freeze resolution. Includes lists of the congressional sponsors and endorsers of the Kennedy-Hatfield Resolution; excerpts from statements in behalf of the resolution; and names and addresses of nuclear-freeze organizations.

Lawler, Philip F. *The Bishops and the Bomb: The Morality of Nuclear Deterrence.* Washington: The Heritage Foundation, 1982.

Lawler, Philip F., ed. *Justice and War in the Nuclear Age.* Lanham, Md.: University Press of America, 1983.

LeFever, Ernest W., and Stephen E. Hunt, eds. *The Apocalyptic Premise: Nuclear Arms Debated.* Washington, D.C.: Ethics and Public Policy Center, 1982.

Lifton, Robert Jay, and Richard Falk. *Indefensible Weapons: The Political and Psychological Case Against Nuclearism.* New York: Basic Books, 1982.

Millar, T. B. *The East-West Strategic Balance.* London: George Allen and Unwin, 1981.

Novak, Michael. "Moral Clarity in the Nuclear Age." *Catholicism in Crisis,* March 1983.

A counter-proposal to the U.S. Roman Catholic bishops' pastoral letter on war and peace. Michael Novak wrote the document, which was endorsed by a group of Roman Catholic lay persons and clergy. The statement rejects pacifism and supports nuclear deterrence.

Polner, Murray, ed. *The Disarmament Catalogue*. New York: The Pilgrim Press, 1982.

Contains extensive bibliography of books on nuclear war and nuclear power and annotated lists of relevant organizations and agencies.

The Role of the Academy in Addressing the Issues of Nuclear War. Geneva, N.Y.: Hobart and William Smith Colleges, 1982.

Russett, Bruce. *The Prisoners of Insecurity: Nuclear Deterrence, the Arms Race, and Arms Control*. San Francisco: W. H. Freeman and Co., 1983.

Scheer, Robert. *With Enough Shovels: Reagan, Bush and Nuclear War*. New York: Random House, 1982.

Schell, Jonathan. *The Fate of the Earth*. New York: Knopf, 1982.

Scoville, Herbert, Jr. *MX: Prescription for Disaster*. Cambridge, Mass.: MIT Press, 1981.

Shannon, Thomas A., ed. *War or Peace? The Search for New Answers*. Maryknoll, N.Y.: Orbis Books, 1980.

Sider, Ronald J., and Darrel J. Brubaker, eds. *Preaching on Peace*. Philadelphia: Fortress Press, 1982.

Sider, Ronald J., and Richard K. Taylor. *Nuclear Holocaust and Christian Hope*. Downers Grove, Ill.: InterVarsity Press, 1982.

Swain, J. Carter. *War, Peace, and the Bible*. Maryknoll, N.Y.:
Orbis Books, 1982.

Vanderhaar, Gerard A. *Christians and Nonviolence in the Nuclear Age: Scripture, the Arms Race, and You*. Mystic, Conn.: Twenty-Third Publications, 1982.

Vernon, Graham D. *Soviet Perceptions of War and Peace*. Washington, D.C.: National Defense University Press, 1981.

Essays by American experts on the Soviet Union; based on Soviet sources.

Wallis, Jim, ed. *Waging Peace: A Handbook for the Struggle to Abolish Nuclear Weapons*. San Francisco: Harper and Row, 1982.

Moral and religious perspectives on the arms race and nuclear weapons. Includes a glossary of terms, a list of "national peace groups," and a map and chart of U.S. nuclear weapons facilities and nuclear power reactors.

Weigel, George. *The Peace Bishops and the Arms Race: Can Religious Leadership Help in Preventing War?* Chicago: World Without War Council, 1982.

Zuckerman, Solly. *Nuclear Illusion and Reality*. New York: Viking Press, 1982.